WHY
SOUTH AFRICA – WHO CARES?

As an international project in 1984/5 the Goodwood Rotary Club sent out nearly 20 000 leaflets to Rotary clubs around the world. The leaflet contained a photograph of crippled children in newly acquired "Rokars" (see pages 20/21) with a message to illustrate that Rotarians in South Africa care as Rotarians do wherever they live.

The response, though not requested, was magnificent from all over the world. Not only were we complimented on our initiative and encouraged, but also called upon to provide more information on Rotary's activities in South Africa.

Fortuitously, our International Committee met with Paul Alberts of The Gallery Press – an international expert in social documentary photography – and the outcome was

SOUTH AFRICA – WHO CARES

We believe there is room for a similar book on Rotarians' efforts in many other parts of the world in a co-ordinated extension of international friendship, goodwill and understanding.

DISTRICT   935

JOHN VAN NIEKERK
PRESIDENT: ROTARY CLUB OF GOODWOOD

SOUTH
AFRICA
WHO
CARES

Text: Ray Hartman
Photography: Paul Alberts, Bee Berman
Patrick Royal, Paul Weinberg
Giselle Wulfsohn
The Gallery Press, Cape Town

SOUTH AFRICA

AFRICA

WHO

CARES

© 1985 The Gallery Press (Pty) Ltd
Set in 10/12pt Helvetica
Lithographic positives by McManus Bros.
Printed on 135 gsm Dukuza Matt Art
by Printpak Books, Cape Town
Book design by Gerhard Last
Final prints by Bee Berman
Cover photograph by Paul Alberts

ISBN 0 620 08980 6

SOUTH AFRICA – WHO CARES was initiated through the International Service Committee of the Goodwood Rotary Club, District 935, South Africa. As information was being gathered, the term kaleidoscope was increasingly used to describe the unfolding picture. This is particularly appropriate as it has become difficult to find even a corner of South African society not influenced by Rotary. So, when paging through SOUTH AFRICA – WHO CARES, we hope that you will take time to savour each scene for, simple as they may initially appear, they have been created by the coupled needs in our society, the love and dedication of those who wanted to help, and the assistance of Rotary in making it possible.

This publication is not intended to be a pretty guidebook – it is intended to show that Rotary is but one of many organisations and groups of people, cutting across all boundaries of race and creed, who do care in South Africa.

There are many people who deserve mention and whose assistance made this book possible. I would like to give their names, but it would call for a small directory. However, their kindness and willingness illuminates, I believe, the images in this work. I thank them collectively for helping to show our common land in service and in community.

John van Niekerk
President, Goodwood Rotary Club.
October 1985

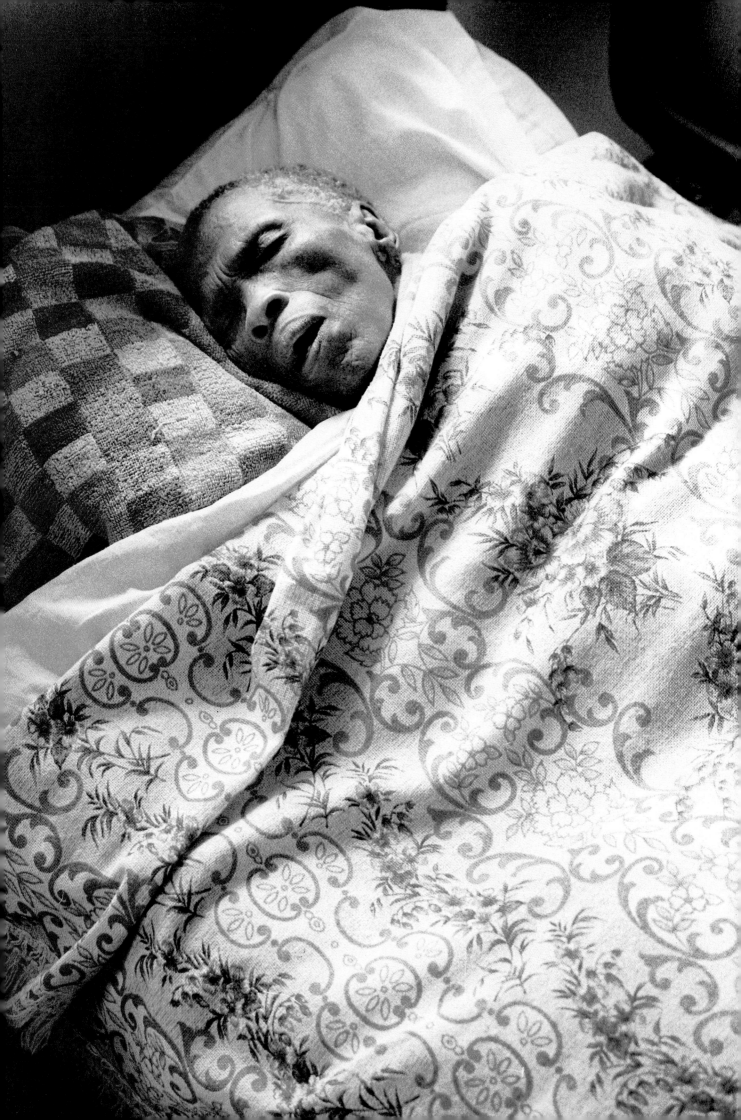

The quality of
a whole civilization
can be judged
by the quality of its care
for the young
and the old.

Preceding page. East London Rotary Club: D. J. Sobey Old Age Home. (Photo: Paul Alberts)

Roodepoort Rotary Club: Coronationville Service Centre. (Photo: Giselle Wulfsohn)

Malnourished child at a Child Welfare clinic on the Cape Flats, another institution benefitting from the Community Chest of the Western Cape.
(Photo: Paul Alberts)

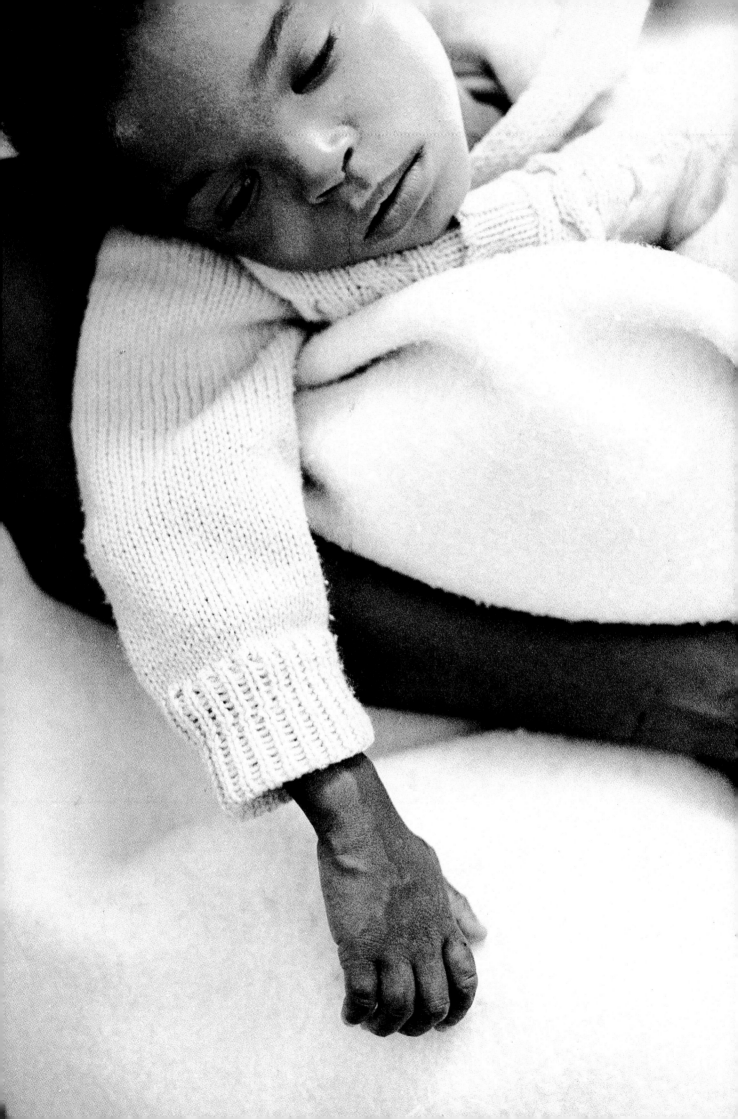

Zerilda Steyn Memorial Home for the Aged, Cape Town. The Community Chest of the Western Cape, founded by Rotary, is one of its major sponsors. (Photo: Paul Alberts)

At the beginning
and towards the end,
possessing nothing perhaps,
but serving no one,
they call on us
for succour.

There are some moments in the history of human affairs when an individual conscience captures for the imagination of mankind our essential predicament: how to pursue fulfilment, comfort and prosperity without sacrificing care and concern for fellow men, women and children.

Such a moment was realised in the United States of America by Mr Paul Harris and became enshrined in the objectives of the Rotary movement world-wide.

In South Africa, Rotarians, guided by the objectives of their founder, endeavour to restore human dignity in areas where society has faltered.

This book serves as a testimony to the role played by Rotary in South Africa over the past six decades in improving the quality of life of innumerable people of all races.

Aliwal North Rotary Club: Local school feeding scheme. (Photo: Paul Alberts)

Matron Zamazulu Nkosi has been in charge of the KwaMashu Polyclinic for the past 18 years. The clinic treats more than 1 000 patients daily and serves seven satellite clinics in a 60 km radius. The frail and elderly people who came for medical care often spoke of hunger and dreadful discomfort. Matron Nkosi knew that the economic pressures of urbanisation and industrialisation had broken traditional tribal life and that the loyalty of family and clan was lost forever, leaving many of the aged to care and fend for themselves. For many of the elderly poor of KwaMashu there is existence rather than life, and existence is a long nightmare. Matron Nkosi says simply that God spoke to her – so she formed her Christian Care Society, and she and her team started going out into the area, visiting the neglected, cleaning, feeding and caring for them.

Durban Berea Rotary Club learned of these plights and the brave efforts of the small team of workers. Inspired, the Club accepted the dream of Matron Nkosi to care for the old and frail in a permanent place and with proper facilities as its Year of the Aged project. In April 1984 the KwaMashu Christian Care Society opened the doors of its old age home and day-care centre – the Zamazulu Nkosi Centre:

- A day care centre for 125 people, cared for and fed daily.
- A meals-on-wheels kitchen serving 300 meals each day to those who would not eat otherwise.
- Accommodation for 32 frail people on a permanent basis.

- A laundry service to the old whose bedding would otherwise rot.
- An eye clinic run by St John's Ambulance.

Many who were left alone in appalling conditions by those who had gone out to work, are now in a community of love and care – rescued from their hunger and maggot-infested mattresses. But more are still uncared for. Future plans provide for the extension of the centre.

As is well known, the principle behind the modest beginning of Rotary in 1905 was the idea that men in business could and should be friends. Two years later the founder became president of the first establishment, the Chicago Rotary Club. That year Rotary took its first step into community service.

Rotary crossed to Canada in 1910 and to England and Ireland in 1911. A constitution was adopted at the 1910 Chicago meeting of 16 clubs with some 1 500 members. There were five objectives, an evolution of the first founding idea, but still somewhat individualistic:

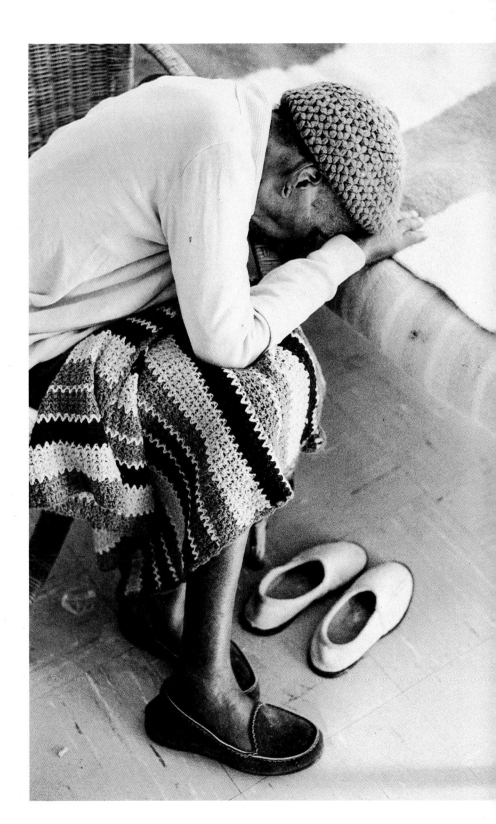

Left: Matron Zamazulu Nkosi.

Right: Durban Berea Rotary Club: Zamazulu Nkosi Centre, KwaMashu. (Photo: Paul Alberts)

- To encourage civic pride and loyalty.
- To promote honourable business methods.
- To advance the business interests of the individual members.
- To organize new clubs.
- To promote the common good of all clubs.

In 1911 the words "He Profits Most Who Serves Best" and "Service, Not Self" were advanced by two speakers at the same convention. They were combined later in the Rotary motto – Service Above Self – He Profits Most Who Serves Best.

The third annual convention changed the name of the organization to The International Association of Rotary Clubs with its five objectives:

- To promote recognition of the worthiness of all legitimate occupations and to use one's occupation as a means of serving society.
- To encourage high ethical standards in business and the professions.
- To increase the efficiency of each member through the exchange of ideas and business methods.
- To promote the "scientizing" of acquaintances as an opportunity for service and as an aid to success.
- To quicken the interest of each member in the public welfare, and to co-operate with others in civic development.

With this constitution a vital link was forged in the evolution of Rotary International's modern constitution, the objects of which were reduced to four, each incorporating the term "service". Friendship, work, occupation and world fellowship, all derive their real meaning from "the ideal of service" to community life.

From here on the pulse of Rotary life quickened. In 1914 the 100th Rotary club was formed in Phoenix, Arizona. Two years later Rotary went to Cuba and in 1921 crossed the equator to Johannesburg, South Africa, to organize the first Rotary club in Africa.

Formation of Rotary in Southern Africa Districts 925, 927, 930, 932 and 935.

1921	1	1939	1	1950	5	1959	9	1970	10	1979	2
1925	5	1940	3	1951	3	1960	7	1971	8	1980	5
1926	1	1943	1	1952	3	1961	8	1972	5	1981	4
1927	1	1944	2	1953	4	1962	3	1973	4	1982	9
1928	1	1945	1	1954	5	1963	1	1974	4	1983	5
1929	1	1946	1	1955	9	1965	5	1975	3	1984	4
1935	1	1947	1	1956	5	1966	6	1976	1	1985	3
1937	1	1948	2	1957	3	1968	3	1977	5		
1938	1	1949	4	1958	7	1969	3	1978	7		

(Photo: Patrick Royal)

The following eloquent sequence was photographed at Fulton School for the Deaf. The Kloof Rotary Club sent a talented teacher of the deaf to the USA to learn the latest techniques. A possible project for the future is an exchange of deaf students, probably with the USA, in addition to the established youth exchange programme. Given a choice, which would you rather lose: sight or hearing? Wherein lies the main weight of information about the world? Is it not in hearing?

(Photos: Patrick Royal)

The Constantia Rotary Club developed the fascinating and successful Rokar from the original Australian concept which worked with a single lever. The twin-lever model is a decisive advance, both mechanically and therapeutically. After producing more than 100 vehicles, the Constantia club transferred the project to the Goodwood Rotary Club.

The human frame and psyche as designed by evolution makes man a swift hunter designed to overcome distance. The whole of our nature requires us to be fundamentally in control of our movements. Unable to discharge the multiple potentialities in the predatory physical inheritance, the child is threatened by psychic collapse. The immobile child is plagued by a deep-seated yearning which corrodes his sense of well-being.

The transformation which a Rokar evokes is miraculous. Sullen children become luminous with the achievement of locomotion – albeit through two-arm levers and wheels. The change is a joy and a wonder to behold.

(Photos: Paul Alberts)

(Photos: Paul Alberts)

The tasks Rotary addresses are as diverse as human thought. The Vanderbijlpark Rotary Club has undertaken many projects, such as a home for alcoholics, blankets for poor black people, a home for the aged and a sun lounge for nursing staff. Another project, the hospital for its local Society for the Prevention of Cruelty to Animals (SPCA), stands high in the affections of the community. Man regards himself as Lord of Creation but it is often in the quality of his compassion for other creatures that his humanity is measured.

In 1488 Bartholomew Diaz, the Portuguese sea captain, on charter to break the Middle East land-bridge trading monopoly with the Orient by seeking a sea route to the wealth in spices and silks, put in at Mossel Bay at the southern end of Africa. As was the custom in those days, he erected a wooden commemoration cross which has long since disappeared. Its stone replica has been celebrated by the Mossel Bay Rotary Club in documentation exchanged with Portugal.

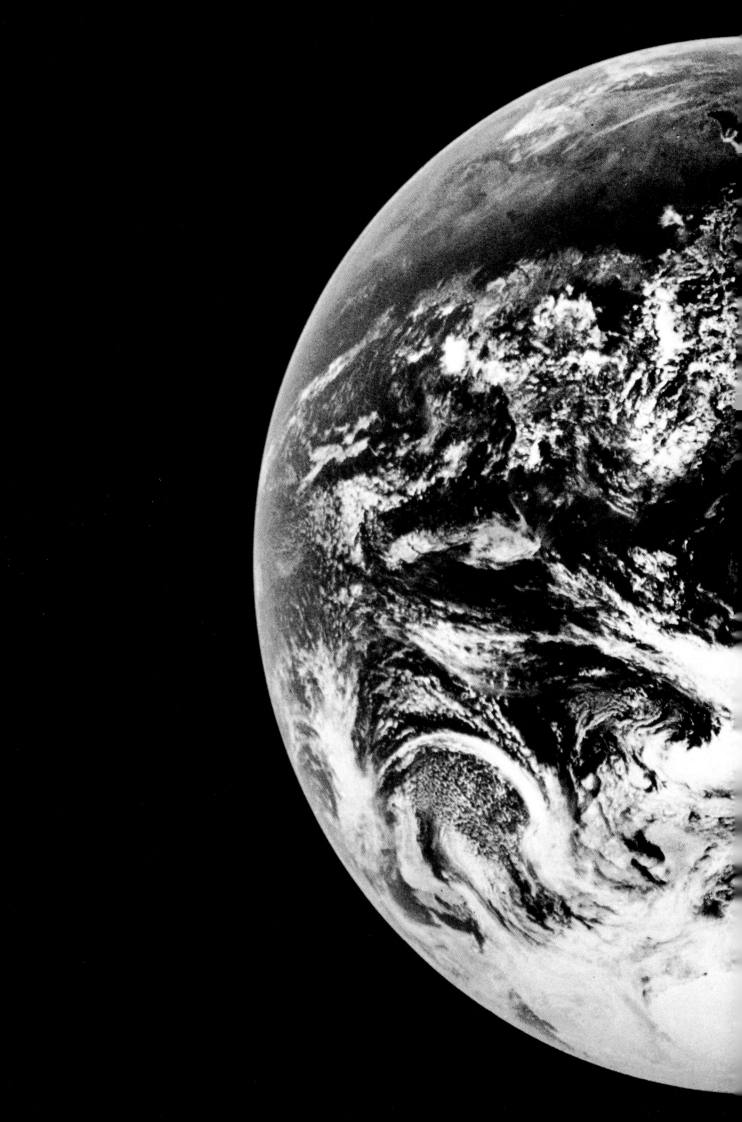

Planet Earth in orbit around the sun, itself in orbit in our galaxy, the Milky Way, shows the continental shield of Africa, floating on the plastic magma of the globe.

On that continental crust more than 400 000 000 Africans of all colours and creeds seek a living in some dignity and a little comfort with immensely unequal endowments.

These lead to inequalities which plunge society into the three great scourges of mankind: poverty, ignorance and disease.

South Africa, in common with the continent, has one of the highest birth rates in the world. People are outstripping the available food supply.

- The parents who will provide this country with a population close to 50 000 000 by the end of the century are alive now.
- Massive unemployment will ensure a continuation of poverty for many millions.
- The right to a meal is inalienable. For the very young its lack can mean the loss of mental potential.

(Photo: NASA)

Far left. Durban South Rotary Club: Their Daily Bread Fund – a project whereby meals are provided on every school day for 30 000 black children at 63 primary schools. (Photo: Patrick Royal)

Above, left and overleaf. The Rotary Club of Cape Town initiated the Cape Flats Distress Association (CAFDA) in 1944. Today this organisation, and the Table Bay Rotary Club assist the Peninsula School Feeding Association (PSFA) by providing bread, soup and, when available, milk to 160 000 primary school children on every school day. The Table Bay club has been involved with PSFA for almost three decades. (Photos: Bee Berman)

Modern society can produce surpluses. The difficulty is to distribute it to the needy. To quote Gandhi: "Earth provides enough to satisfy everyman's need, but not everyman's greed."

One spoon of milk powder at a meal can make a child resilient to protein-deficiency disease: the difference between radiance and dullness.

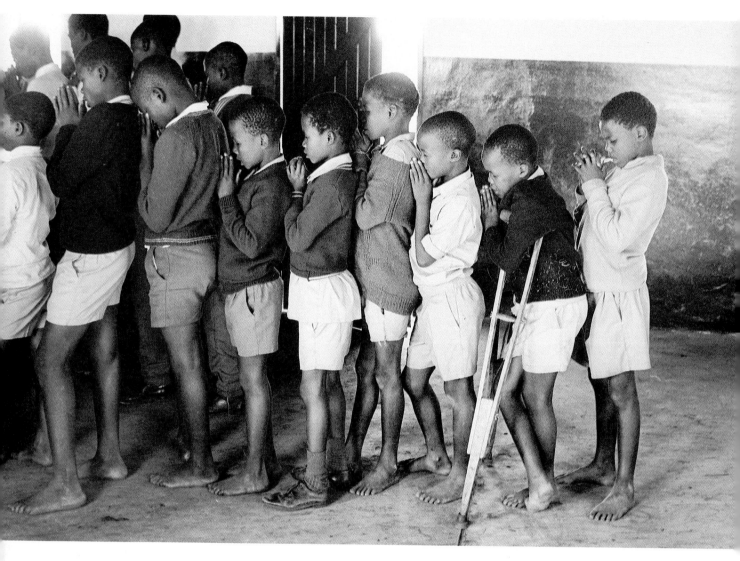

If poverty can be held in check there is still ignorance to be overcome. But no culture, no matter how deprived, is ever 'ignorant'. It is often rich in heritage, even enviable in folklore, lacking perhaps mainly in knowledge leading to modernization.

■ Modernity is acquired. It is the Westernization of beliefs founded in superstition. It is often a mistake.

■ The path to modern thinking need not follow the route of industrialization. But whatever good or bad attends the process, a modernizing education, as things stand at present, is essential for some degree of affluence.

Above all else the farm school produces basic literacy and numeracy as the essential preparation for productivity. Without the latter there can be no improvement in wages and therefore less chance of breaking out of the cycle of poverty.

The education available is often limited. Even so, parents will suffer almost any sacrifice to secure as much as possible of it for their children.

Beaufort West Rotary Club: Built additional classrooms at a local black school to enable senior pupils to complete their schooling from home. (Photo: Paul Alberts)

Eshowe Rotary Club: Together with the Eshowe Christian Action Group of Zululand this club already provided 200 classrooms at farm schools in KwaZulu on an assisted self-help basis involving the local communities. (Photo: Patrick Royal)

"Early learning" has revolution-
ized educational thinking in the
past three decades. If the very
young are caught up in a creative
teaching environment it seems
the human brain is galvanized
into learning activity which does
not easily subside.

Rosebank Rotary Club: Pre-primary school in Alexandra, Johannesburg. (Photo: Paul Weinberg)

Claremont Rotary Club: Alpha
Creche, Hanover Park, Cape
Town. (Photo: Bee Berman)

Investment in this area has an enormously stimulating "multiplier" effect. Caught early and nurtured, the child's innate thirst for the excitement of learning may more easily become a life-long habit.

Rosebank Rotary Club: Pre-primary school in Alexandra, Johannesburg. (Photo: Paul Weinberg)

Edenvale Rotary Club and Johannesburg Main Reef Rotary Club:
Provided beds at the Ezibileni
Home for Crippled Black Children,
a project of the Germiston Cripple
Care Association. (Photo: Paul
Weinberg)

The lingering nightmare of disease and the wasted lives which follow if medical help is not available, is perhaps the most evil of the three scourges afflicting mankind.

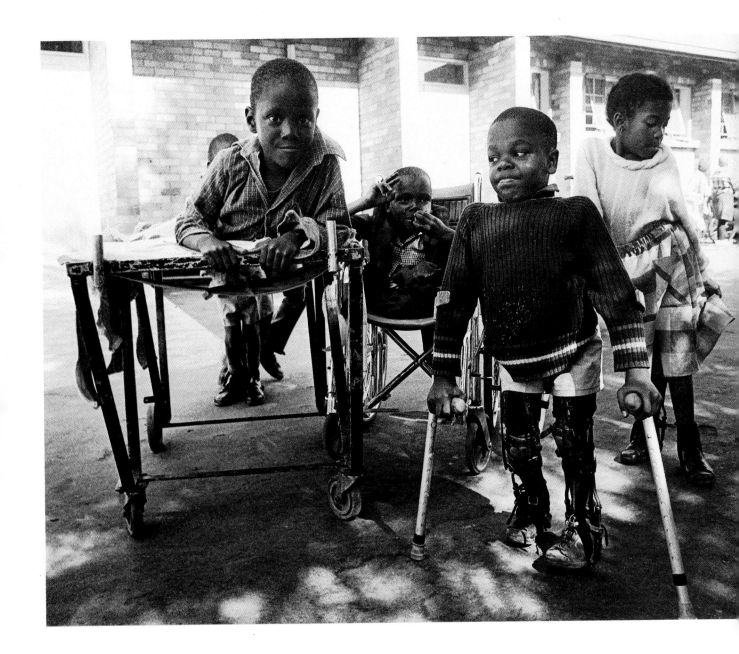

"CHARGES FOR OUT-PATIENTS: As we are working in a very poor area and the welfare of the people is more important than the price of medicine, we do not put much emphasis on payment at our out-patients' clinic. If a patient can afford it we charge R2,00 but there is no charge for return visits or extra medicines." Quote from report on St. Brendan's Clinic and Nursing Home at the Catholic Mission, Dwars River, Bandelierskop in Lebowa.

(Photos: Paul Alberts)

STATISTICS FOR 1981:
Number of patients treated at out-patients' clinic, of which about 40 percent suffer from pellagra and malnourishment: 14 641

Number of patients treated at ante-natal clinic: 2 839

Number of admissions: 1 111

Number of deliveries: 1 096

"The present labour ward is merely a corridor between the night nurses' room and one of the post-natal wards. It cannot be kept sterile. The ante-natal ward is too small for chairs or bedside lockers. The women use an outdoors WC and bath in the open. The roofs are leaking, the timber is rotting. The walls are damp and will not hold paint. The plumbing and electrical wiring have to be replaced. The sewage system is haphazard, inadequate and often blocked. In fact, it is a health hazard. St. Brendan's needs a completely new building."

The Pietersburg Rotary Club has adopted St. Brendan's Clinic as an on-going project. Buildings are being constructed with bricks made by the people. A happy spin-off is the possibility of generating cash-income from brick-making when their own needs are met. St. Brendan's reaffirms the innate genius of a people to help themselves if given the means.

The cost of nursing the sick back to health calls for great expenditure in infra-structure – buildings, apparatus, staff, etc. Some illness is inescapable, but much can be avoided by preventive medicine.

The ideal is to teach modern ideas of hygiene through improved education and so sidestep the sickness that follows from ignorance of causative agents.

Only eight years after its charter was granted, the Springs Rotary Club began a tuberculosis and dental health survey for all races in 1943. This historic and far-sighted work eventually became the South African National Tuberculosis Association (SANTA) and has touched the lives of tens of thousands since its formation in 1958.

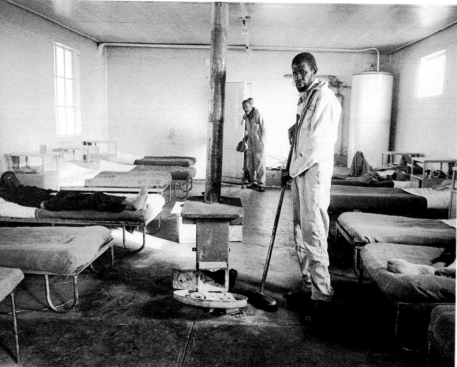

Today the Benoni Van Ryn and the Springs Rotary clubs continue this tradition by refurbishing and upgrading the early barrack-like, industrialized wards of the first era in TB medication. Many clubs from District 930 are involved in this major project transforming the stark, if sanitary, interior to the sparkle and stimulation of TV. This is a step towards treating the whole person rather than the patient.

South Africa has one of the highest TB rates in the world. Most countries, including the industrialized Western economies, have an uneven distribution of health.

Those who suffer from ill-health are not always the poor. Miners and some factory workers, for instance, are stricken by and die of lung diseases as part of work hazards. But TB stands as a clear question mark calling to account a society's nutritional levels. Vulnerability to TB begins with malnourishment, although food hygiene helps.

Preventive thinking and planning is the least costly in infrastructure.

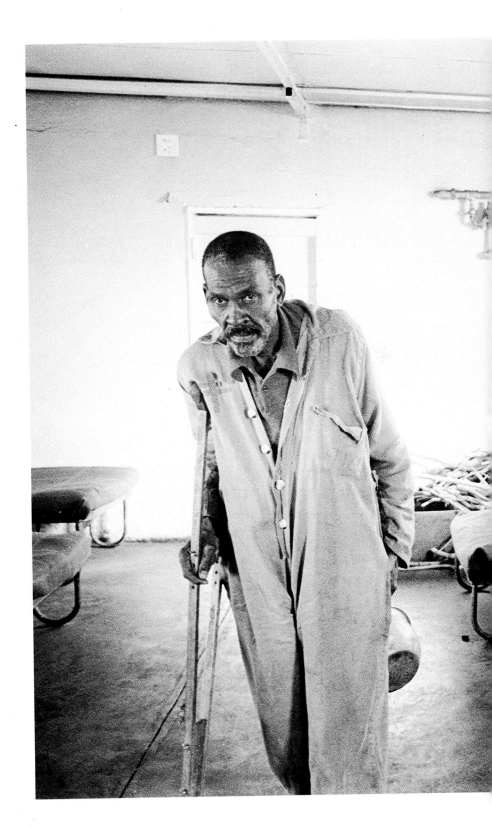

(Photos: Paul Weinberg)

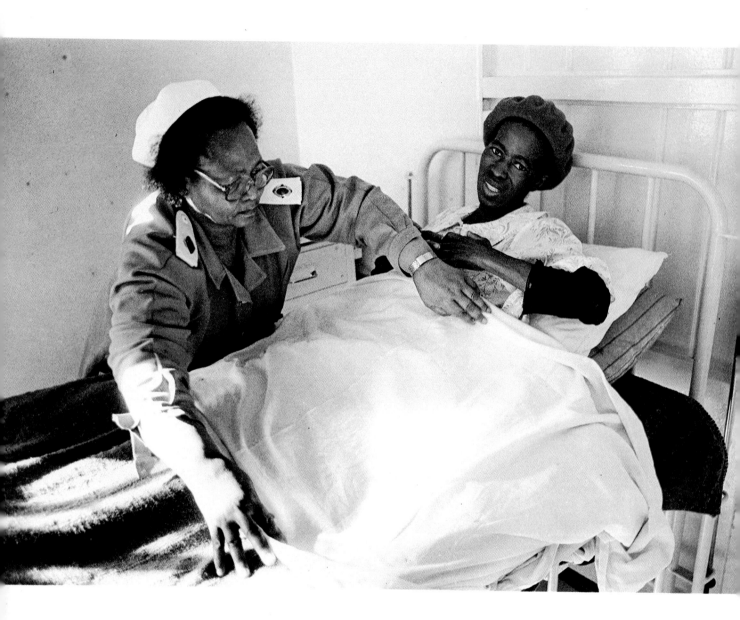

All that will ever be known about the world resides in the human head. Dimly as they may have perceived the world 1 000 000 years ago, the Australopithecines sharpening their stone tools in the area between Potchefstroom and Nairobi, conceived their view of nature in their heads.

In 10 000 years, when Mars has been inhabited for thousands of years by Earthlings (called Martians), man's knowledge of the Cosmos and its structure – a mystery to even the most advanced imagination now – will be constructed in the human cranium.

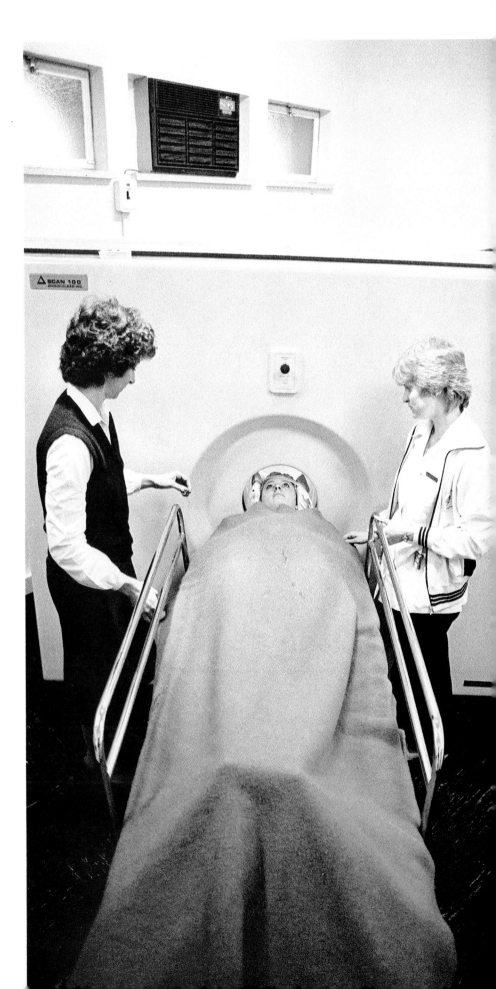

Right and overleaf: Arcadia Rotary Club in East London donated a C.A.T. scanner to the Frere Hospital. (Photos: Paul Alberts)

Injury to the head can be our most vital concern. Mapping the cerebral cortex in the human skull to determine the nature and extent of injury is now a significantly simpler task. Computerised Axial Tomographic (C.A.T.) scanning of the head makes this form of high-technology medicine a routine practice. People suffering brain injury in East London, Ciskei and Transkei had formerly to be flown 300 km to Port Elizabeth or 1 000 km to Cape Town.

A second generation C.A.T. scanner which cost R93 000 in 1984 was donated by the Arcadia Rotary Club, East London. As a result Frere Hospital now has a resident neuro-surgeon to help ensure our view of the world remains 'intact'.

(Photo: Paul Alberts)

Charter 976 is an historic document.
Apart from Johannesburg,
all other clubs on the African continent
have been admitted to membership
in Rotary International.
Johannesburg was admitted to
the International Association of
Rotary Clubs before the change
of name in 1922.

The history of Rotary's five districts in Southern Africa, in the main, lies scattered in the projects its ever-growing list of clubs has undertaken. No central archive has as yet assembled the documents reflecting the many-faceted history of an organization so intimately concerned with the social fabric of South Africa. A formal history of Rotary is not feasible in the short term. Useful accounts have been written by dedicated workers, yet they are often bare-bone histories of dates or compilations of anecdotes, valuable to the club concerned but local in interest.

There are a few exceptions where histories have had the

Louis Trichardt Rotary Club: Tons of firewood is consumed annually by the average African family. Deforestation is inevitable. This club initiated a reforestation project in which the community is actively involved. (Photo: Paul Alberts)

The Spirit of Rotary is an ambulance with a difference: it is a sophisticated aircraft used to transport patients to main medical centres in the Cape. All clubs in Rotary District 935 contributed financially to this project. (Photo: Bee Berman)

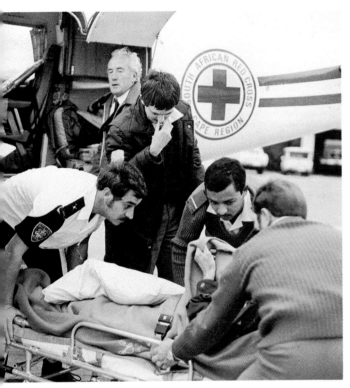

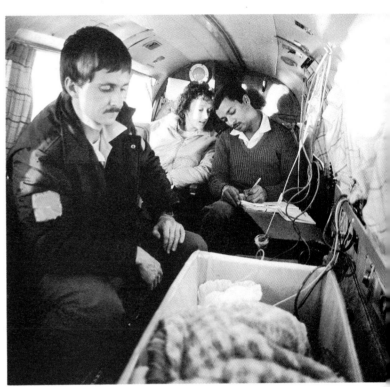

happy combination of scholarship and a lucky archive plus some members with long memories. On these we have drawn for a somewhat impressionistic sketch of Rotary history.

The first Rotary club outside the Anglo-Saxon community of countries was in Africa. To Johannesburg in one of its most turbulent decades, Charter number 976 was granted on July 1, 1921 to set the Rotary wheel in motion towards a future that has captivated the world's imagination.

Two generations later the wheel of history has come full circle and Rotary finds itself compassionately involved in Johannesburg East Rotary Club in association with the clubs of Johannesburg Main Reef and Johannesburg South established the Avalon Home for paraplegics. (Photo: Giselle Wulfsohn)

Worcester Rotary Club: Established the Worcester Cripple Care Association. (Photo: Bee Berman)

another decade of service to a community in upheaval.

Only seven months after the founding meeting, "the progress of the Rotary Club of Johannesburg came to a jarring halt". (p.23 K. Buchanan, The First 60 Years: A Saga of Service.) Some members of the Johannesburg Rotary Club were involved on the

side of the authorities during the 1922 Gold Miners' Strike, which erupted into revolt and civil war. The club's Monday meetings were abandoned in the turmoil of open insurrection and daily casualties, to be resumed only months later. Although white miners were fighting capitalism and the Government, and casual-

ties were mainly white, the dislocations of the period and its parallels with the strife of the 1980s are remarkable.

The first community service of a Rotary club on the African continent was the support and organization of established – but waning – Sunday night concerts at the Johannesburg General

Hospital. These live performances were supplemented by Wednesday night gramophone concerts in the cancer ward. A Charter member, Mr Oliver Hoskings, spent 10 years expanding these concerts to other institutions, and before his resignation in 1931 persuaded Rotary to buy a projector to use in the cancer

Raadzaal Rotary Club (Bloemfontein): Established the Olea Interim Home for patients receiving treatment for cancer. This project received a Significant Achievement Award. (Photo: Paul Alberts)

A family being interviewed by a social worker of Child Welfare at a clinic near Cape Town. This organisation is one of many benefitting from the Community Chest of the Western Cape, originally established by the Cape Town Rotary Club. (Photo: Paul Alberts)

ward on Wednesday nights.

The next decade found another devotee of the Rotary Service Committee, Mr Thomas Griffin, who laid the foundation of musical and film entertainment to the ill so securely that further pianos were donated to Johannesburg General and new film

projectors acquired. Just before the advent of TV "Griffs' Service Committee" was providing an astonishing 500 film shows annually. (p.28 op cit.) There was a time in Johannesburg when every home of the chronically ill, all old age homes and every orphanage and children's home enjoyed at least a monthly and

often a weekly film show or concert.

While face-to-face compassionate service among patients, the aged and orphans was well-structured for the time, larger, more complex issues were being studied in Rotary. In 1925 when Durban, Port Elizabeth, Cape Town and Pietermaritzburg were being formed, issues were addressed by Rotary Johannesburg that would reshape the conscience of the whole society.

In the history referred to, Mr Kelsey Buchanan, Past-President, Past-District Governor and past Director of Rotary International, reports that "Johannesburg Club has several times ven-

Durban Rotary Club: Several clinics in remote parts of KwaZulu, Natal, were provided with two-way radios linking them to the Prince Mshiyeni Memorial Hospital in Umlazi. (Photo: Paul Alberts)

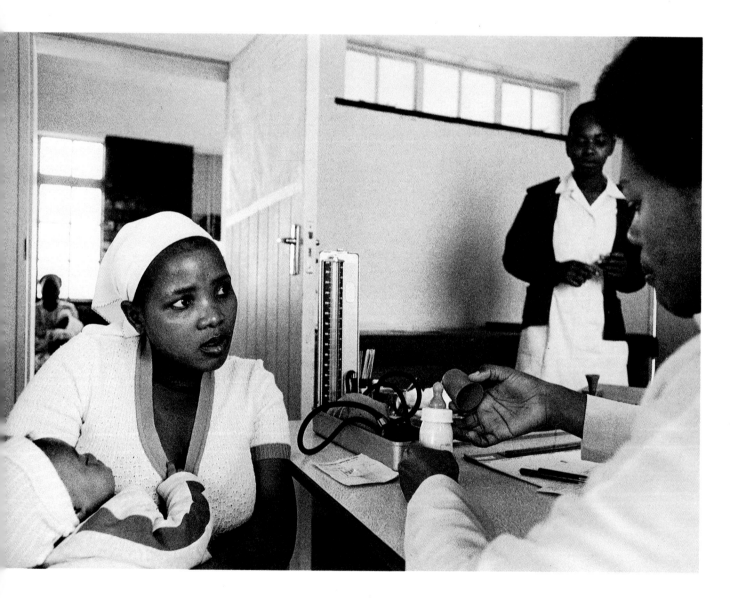

Springs Rotary Club: Continued involvement with a TB hospital near Benoni. A tuberculosis and dental health survey by this club in 1943 eventually led to the formation in 1958 of the South African Tuberculosis Association (SANTA). (Photo: Paul Weinberg)

tured into the wider field of injustices and disabilities being suffered by Africans countrywide. . ." (p.57 op cit.)

As a result of earlier investigations the first District Conference in Africa, held in Cape Town in April 1927, heard several resolutions seeking district action on matters such as the pass

laws. In the conference of the following year the Government was asked in the name of Rotary to provide health services for black people in urban and rural areas.

The Non-European Affairs Committee of Rotary, Johannesburg, acting in concert with a number of public bodies in deputation to the Secretary for

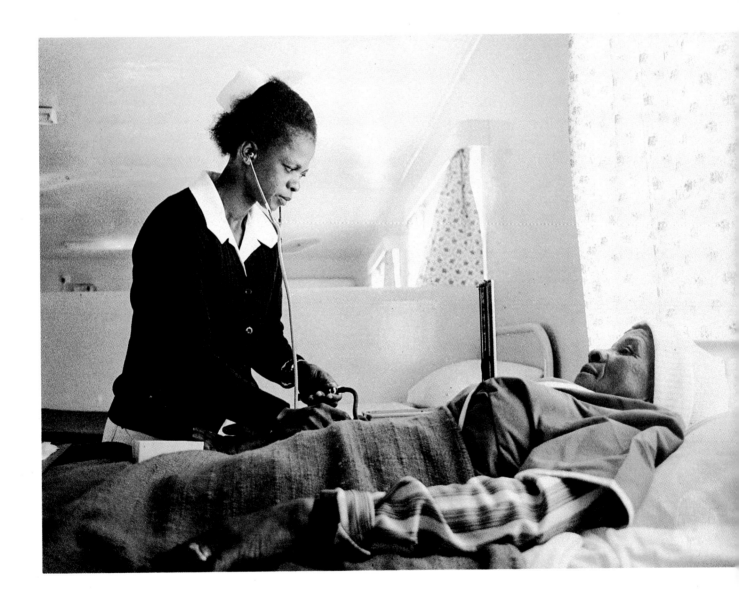

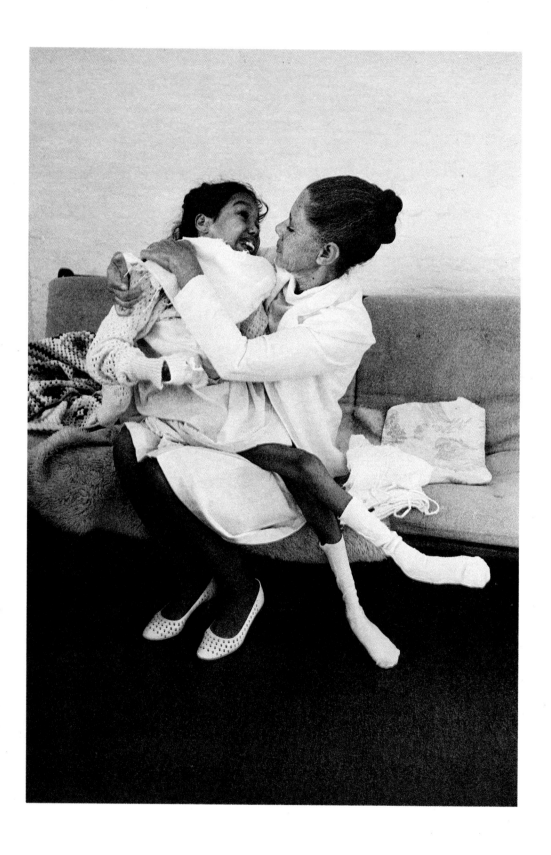

Durban Umgeni Rotary Club: Established the Cheshire Home for Mentally Handicapped Coloured Children. (Photo: Paul Alberts)

Pretoria 6 Rotary Club: Provided funds for a training unit for the blind at the Rehabilitation Centre, Pretoria, where they are trained in the use of typewriters and other office equipment. (Photo: Paul Alberts)

Native Affairs, urged in 1930 the use of a simplified pass system for Africans. (The 'pass system' is documentation which must be carried at all times and which restricts the movement of blacks and hence their ability to seek and find work.)

The Secretary evidently agreed entirely, but new legislation in Parliament the same year affected the issue and the Rotary proposals were shelved.

In 1933 – and for the next five years – Johannesburg Rotary commenced an action relating to legal process in South Africa which successfully ended in a profound improvement in legal representation for both poor

black and white citizens. The Transvaal Law Society at first conceded to Rotary the need for a panel of attorneys to act pro Deo in African cases, but Rotary wanted more. The club persuaded Professor Hoernle of the University of the Witwatersand to chair a meeting of the Department of Justice, the Law Society, the Bar Council and the Legal Clerks Associations, plus the Rotary Committee. A delegation from this meeting was chosen to meet the Secretary for Justice. Mr H A Damant represented the club.

Arising out of these deliberations the Prisoner's Friend in South Africa was instituted in

Pretoria East Rotary Club: Built a bowling green for blind bowlers in Sunnyside. (Photo: Paul Alberts)

Germiston North Rotary Club: Donates guide dogs to the South African Guide Dogs Association (Photo: Giselle Wulfsohn)

Durban Berea Rotary Club: Raised funds for the building of the Zamazulu Nkosi Centre, KwaMashu. (Photo: Paul Alberts)

1938. His role was to interview all awaiting trial prisoners and to decide on the granting of legal aid. His decision was given to a member of Rotary who passed the subject to a panel of attorneys and advocates willing to act pro Deo for the accused. Out of this procedure grew the Legal Aid System. Set up in 1940, it in-augurated free legal representation for poor whites and Africans.

The readiness and willingness of the first Rotary club in Africa to apply "the ideal of service by every Rotarian to his personal, business and community life", and "the development of ac-

Goodwood Rotary Club: Established the Handyman's Scheme which provides employment for pensioners. (Photo: Bee Berman)

Somerset West Rotary Club: Established Vonke House for the Aged. (Photo: Bee Berman)

quaintance as an opportunity for service" are underscored again and again in the experiences of the Non-European Affairs Committee during the formative years of 1923-1950. It is clear that Rotary was scrutinizing and clarifying for itself what was intended in the concept "community life" in the South Africa of that period.

A generation later, re-examination of the boundaries of community life may well suggest new definitions of "service".

One problem that straddles both generations is that of urban slums. Combined with one of the most severe droughts of the century, the Depression years of 1929-33 drove Africans out of ru-

ral areas into cities where low wages and lack of housing created appalling slums. The advent of World War II drew even more migrants to the cities and municipalities found the burden of subsidised African housing beyond their means. In 1948, a crisis was created by the Johannesburg municipality's declara-tion that it could no longer carry the mounting losses in the provision of low-cost housing. The Government refused any increase in subsidy, calling instead on industry and commerce to share the expense.

Johannesburg Rotary Club involved itself and a report to the Non-European Affairs Commit-

Johannesburg Rotary Club: Established Rotary Park, a housing project for the aged comprising 100 units. (Photo: Giselle Wulfsohn)

Goodwood Rotary Club: Organise tours for the aged on a regular basis, travelling as far afield as the Kruger National Park. (Photo: Paul Alberts)

tee found that some 10 000 self-built mud-brick houses had been erected in Moroka. Instead of the expected slum, Rotarian Mr John Cope reported pride of ownership and clean, well-cared for dwellings, in spite of the poor building materials. Moreover, there was less crime in Moroka than in the municipal, subsidised

housing scheme of Orlando. All of this has a contemporary ring.

The Rotary Committee suggested that an unskilled black person could build his own three-roomed house for about 50 Pounds compared to the cost of 200 Pounds for the municipality. Rotary called for the first five names out of a waiting list of

15 000, and Mr Aaron Sibiya, a bus conductor, built his own house with sun-dried soil bricks for 50 Pounds, 19 shillings. This, and continuing experimental building at Pimville, became the basis for a report on self-help housing to the Johannesburg City Council. Rotarians persuaded the Association of Building Societies to consider advancing up to 1 000 000 Pounds for self-help housing – that was funds for almost 20 000 houses. However, for complex reasons, Africans were not interested and the scheme collapsed.

Rotary ideas concerning African housing were investigated by Sir Ernest Oppenheimer in

Estcourt Rotary Club: Established the Veld and Vlei Outward Bound Youth Survival Course. (Photos: Paul Alberts)

1947 in the Alex McPhail scheme and incorporated in African housing on the Free State gold mines.

The remarkable record of Johannesburg Rotary's Non-European Affairs Committee in areas today considered to have a "political" connotation indicates how climates of opinion alter. A reversal of pattern appears to be in the offing.

The sensitivity of Rotary nowadays to "politics" by even indirect and remote association may be explained by the traumatic events surrounding a press report, Johannesburg Rotary and Dr H F Verwoerd, the Prime Minister. As Mr Kelsey Buchanan

Boksburg Rotary Club: Established Bokkie Park for city-born children to play in and learn about animals in a park-like environment. (Photos: Paul Alberts)

records (pp 148-149 op. cit.) Rotary International's President, Mr Charles Pettengill, "was the victim of a breach of journalistic etiquette which almost disrupted the Rotary movement in Southern Africa". Asked to comment on the introduction of a law which allowed people to be detained for 90 days without trial for allegedly political reasons, Mr Pettengill rightly refused comment on the grounds of interference in the politics of another country. The press interview over, the journalist invited Mr Pettengill – who was about to board a flight at Jan Smuts Airport – to have coffee with other Rotarians present. In casual

Port Elizabeth Rotary Club: Mr T MacQuhae, an engineer by training, started the Toys for Joy project many years ago. Several other clubs have since adopted this project. Mr MacQuhae is a recipient of a Paul Harris Award. (Photo: Paul Alberts)

Kimberley South Rotary Club: Established a playground at the Jannie Brink Training Centre for Mentally Retarded Children. (Photo: Paul Alberts)

Durban South Rotary Club: Built a miniature town (Minitown) on Durban's beachfront in conjunction with Round Table No.2 to provide an ongoing source of funds, for welfare purposes, from entrance fees. (Photo: Paul Alberts)

conversation the reporter asked for his comment on the law in his capacity as lawyer rather than that of Rotary President. "As a lawyer, I wouldn't go along with it," he replied and turned to other matters.

Prominent headlines the next day quoted the remark. Two days later, Dr Verwoerd in a major speech declared that steps to control Rotary might be taken if it was shown to be interfering in the policies of government. Most of the members of the Piet Retief Rotary Club resigned in protest, as did many other Afrikaans-speaking members of many Rotary clubs. The next day, over a cup of tea, District Governor

Middelburg Rotary Club: Organise an annual school art competition. Inge Brandmuller, a previous winner. (Photo: Paul Alberts)

Kimberley Rotary Club: Assisted with the establishment of an Interact Club at the Elizabeth Conradie School for the Physically Handicapped. (Photo: Paul Alberts)

Jack Boswell gave Dr Verwoerd the correct explanation, which was accepted. Two days later at the opening of a dam in Natal, the Prime Minister publicly announced he had been given a true account and was content with Rotary in South Africa. Most Rotarians who had resigned, returned.

Although the position has changed with the years, and may change again, the record of the Johannesburg Rotary Club shows that many leading politicians spoke as guests on subjects which today would be labelled as "political" or controversial. Indeed, official requests to use Rotary as a plat-

form for launching major policy initiatives, were made by notable politicians. Dr Verwoerd, as Minister of Native Affairs, at a Rotary function gave one of the first intimations of the plan for "Bantu Homelands". Mr Tielman Roos, in an earlier era, chose the club's forum to advance his attack on the Government after re-

signing from the Supreme Court Bench which led to South Africa coming off the gold standard and eventually restoring its economic position in the crisis of the international Depression and the drought at home.

The Rotary Club Board knew that at any time the opposing point of view to any issue could

Durban Musgrave Rotary Club: A basic course for black businessmen was launched in 1980. Two years later the club was awarded the Rotary International Significant Achievement Award for this project. (Photo: Robert Gorneman)

Johannesburg North-Central Rotary Club: Established a road safety training centre at the Forest Town School for Cerebral Palsied Children. (Photo: Giselle Wulfsohn)

be stated from its platform. It was a free exchange of ideas which called for openness of debate among business and professional personalities. The times called for it to be so.

The fission of founding clubs by cession of territory to new clubs is a feature of Rotary's growth in South Africa. Where

from 1921-1954 there was one Rotary club in Johannesburg, 13 clubs now exist to serve the expanding population and extended needs.

The first Rotary club in Africa served as a model for much future inspiration, and perhaps rightly so, because its sympathies were not only broadly

based but finely tuned to the existing needs and sometimes crises of a rapidly industrializing society.

Thus, for example, the entire cripple care organisation in South Africa (soon to be re-named the Association for the Physically Disabled) is a memorial to Mr J C Merkin, a charter member and, by his longevity, the last Charter member of Rotary Johannesburg.

The school which carries his name is unique. It was the first day-school for disabled black children, the first to provide bus-sing to and from school, the first in dual-language teaching, the first to provide occupational

Hermanus Rotary Club: Contri-buted to the establishment of the Camphill School near Hermanus. (Photo: Bee Berman)

Durbanville Rotary Club: Supplied the Alpha Camphill Village at Malmesbury with milking machines and work benches. (Photo: Bee Berman)

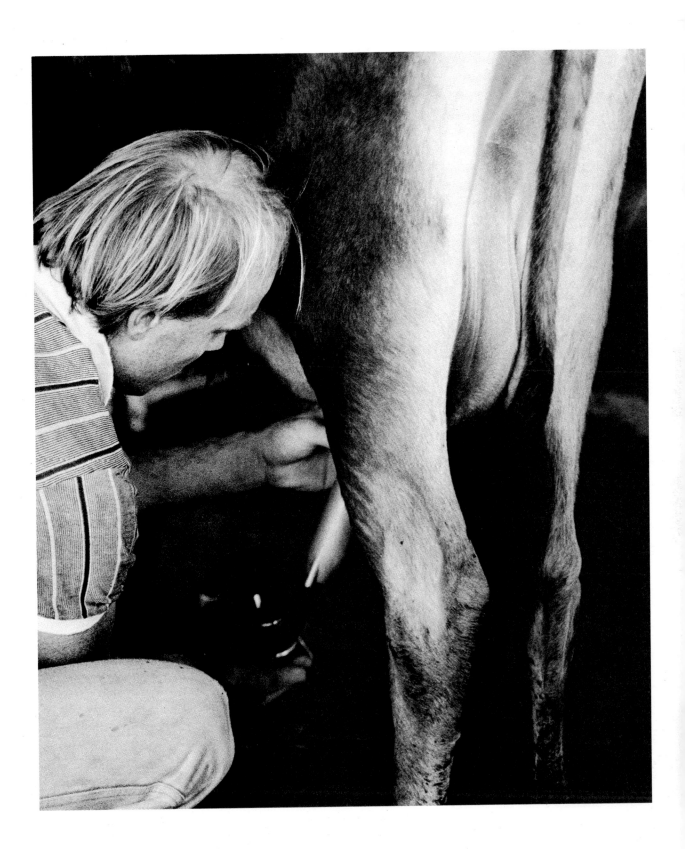

Arcadia Rotary Club and Gately Rotary Club (East London): Involvement with the Malcomess Children's Home led to the refurbishing of dormitories and the general up-grading of the Home. (Photo: Paul Alberts)

Port Shepstone Rotary Club: Initiated the construction of the Southern Natal Commercial High School. (Photo: Patrick Royal)

therapy and physiotherapy, and so on. Importantly, it is totally maintenance-free.

With the arrival of TV a scheme was evolved in the Johannesburg Rotary Club which led to the installation of 100 colour TV sets in institutions throughout South Africa, acting through local clubs. It was through this

club that the British 'Outward Bound' survival school was transplanted to South Africa to become the Veld and Vlei Adventure Trust. This organisation has grown into a vital leadership-training school for all races.

In 1955/56 Johannesburg Rotary Club became the first club in South Africa to operate under a

Durban Port Natal Rotary Club: The Port Natal Community Centre provides day-care for 70 children of working parents in the Point area of Durban. (Photo: Paul Alberts)

Rondebosch Rotary Club: Provided jungle-jims at Justin Street Creche, Hanover Park, near Cape Town. (Photo: Bee Berman)

Rosebank Rotary Club: Established a pre-primary school in Alexandra, Johannesburg. (Photo: Paul Weinberg)

registered welfare organisation number – 2 303 – and was also the first to create a separate Fund-Raising Committee in an attempt to relieve committees of this essential chore. This occurred after an intense debate of some five years' duration on the question as to whether Rotary was more a service than a fund-

raising organisation. The mutuality of these two aspects to Rotary endeavour was convincingly demonstrated when Johannesburg, North Central, Northcliff and Sandton Rotary clubs combined in response to a plea from Bophuthatswana to provide radio linkage between the main hospitals and clinics in

remote rural areas. Poor rural telephone connections put patients at grave risk in emergencies when clinics tried to raise the hospitals for urgent medical advice and met with communication delays. In very short order, trouble-free sets were designed and manufactured for use by non-radio staff, masts were

erected, two radio frequencies were allocated by the Post Office and the problem of getting life-saving advice through to clinics from doctors and specialists was solved. Durban Rotary Club passed this innovation on to the Prince Mshiyeni Memorial Hospital in Umlazi and clinics in the remote parts of KwaZulu.

Pinetown Rotary Club: Established the Marianhill Club, also known as the Old Mill Club, in conjunction with the Marianhill Mission Institute. Sport facilities and a creche have been provided for the more than 5 000 people who frequent the club monthly. (Photo: Paul Alberts)

Johannesburg East Rotary Club: Supports a scheme – the Soweto

Child Minders – to provide care for children of working mothers. (Photo: Paul Alberts)

Durban Rotary Club: Umbumbulu Central Clinic, one of several in remote parts of KwaZulu, Natal, where two-way radios were provided linking them to the Prince Mshiyeni Memorial Hospital in Umlazi. (Photo: Paul Alberts)

The fine-grained nature of the Rotarian passion for service also embraces larger social issues. At the time of the Soweto riots of 1976/77, when civil unrest was sparked off by the poor quality of education, Rotary set out quietly to help raise the academic standard of 3 000 black teachers. The first problem was that re-training was conducted by extra-mural tuition in the evening, working by candle-light. There was no electricity at that time. With the help of the Benoni van Ryn, Roodepoort and Rosebank Rotary clubs, 72 gas lamps of 300 candle-power were provided. The success rate was phenomenal. Numbers grew to 9 000 tea-

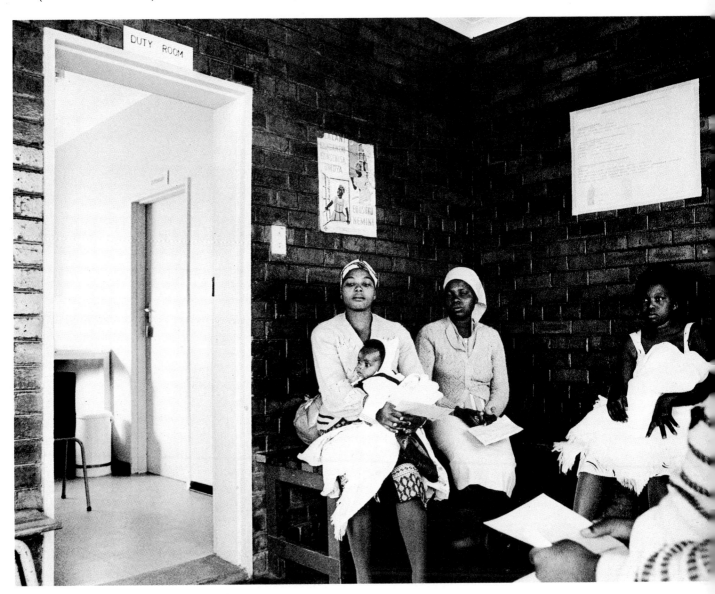

chers and adults seeking night classes in 1978, to 20 000 in 1980 and throughout the country to 50-60 000 by mid-1980, and are still growing.

It does not matter whose finger is on the light switch as long as there is light. The ability of Rotary to be inventive and respon-sive to the needs of the times is rooted in the great variety of in-telligence marshalled in the clubs nationwide. And the ca-pacity to transmit a shared expe-rience swiftly among so many makes it unique among service organisations. There are almost 8 000 members in nearly 200 clubs from all professions and

Left and right: Johannesburg East Rotary Club in association with the Johannesburg Main Reef and Jo-hannesburg South clubs estab-lished the Avalon Home for para-plegics. (Photos: Giselle Wulfsohn)

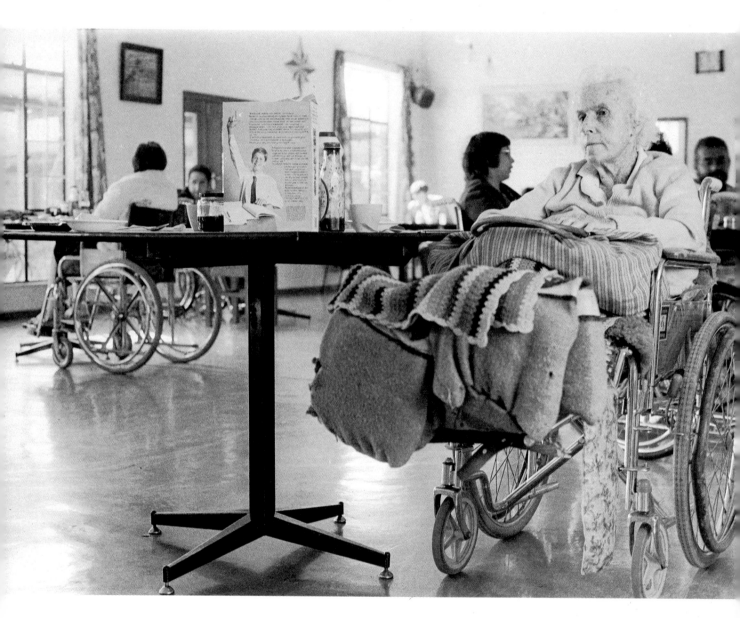

Bottom: Edenvale Rotary Club: Raising funds for the donation of beds to the Ezibileni Home for Crippled Black Children. (Photo: Paul Weinberg)

major organisations. This is a resource unmatched by any agency in the country.

It is sometimes the case that there are resources available, but dormant in society, which need only a degree of know-how to release them in the right direction. Locked away in the coffers of bureaucracies and their budgets are funds which can be induced to flow if certain conditions are met. The conditions are often complex, and finding the right combination to unlock the capital calls for a particular flair and some skill in negotiations with the authorities.

It would appear that the Table Bay Rotary Club has nurtured a

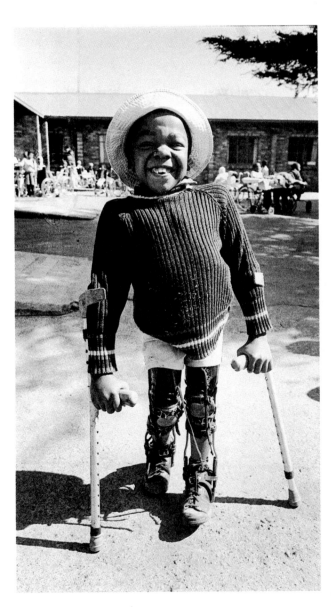

tradition of expertise dating back to the 1950's which enables them to mobilise municipal funds imaginatively. A good illustration of this tradition is their triumph of co-ordination with the Cape Town City Council in creating the Paarden Eiland Park. In the all too familiar industrialized fringe of the city, lacking in amenities, a green lung was created from an industrial dump. Where factory workers were confined to waste-land yards during work breaks, they now relax on a lush green sward surrounded by trees – a living space to restore the spirit. Much grit and determination were expended in getting provin-cial and local authorities to make

Cape of Good Hope Rotary Club: Contributes to the Ocean View Centre for the Handicapped near Cape Town. The club has also equipped a children's playground at this Centre. (Photo: Bee Berman)

East London Rotary Club: Established the D.J. Sobey Old Age Home. (Photo: Paul Alberts)

the necessary R100 000 available for the conversion. Table Bay Rotary Club paid for the trees and park furniture.

Collaborating with the Chamber of Industry and the Chamber of Commerce, Table Bay Club also persuaded the City Council to up-grade several housing estates which had be-come depressed. Rotary expertise and influence brought about extensive renovations in, for instance, Maitland Garden Village. Here the priorities were re-roofing and re-wiring whole streets of houses. The mobilisation of municipal resources done, Rotary accepted responsibility for establishing a creche and

Roodepoort Rotary Club: Donated a bus to transport the elderly to the Coronationville Service Centre, where they are entertained and involved in craft and hobby activities. (Photo:Giselle Wulfsohn)

Johannesburg Rotary Club: Established Rotary Park, a housing project for the aged. (Photo: Giselle Wulfsohn)

recreational areas in the Village.

There is a singular satisfaction in cultivating the art of multiplying slender resources by marshalling the power of, for instance, local government spending. The Rotary Club of Table Bay has shown determination in a sensitive manner. To the poorer communities, overwhelmed by the rules of officialdom, the results have been sheer magic.

ROTARY FUTURES OF THE PAST

Thinking and discussion in many Rotary committees have in the past ranged far beyond their times.

- Rotarian Mr L I Venables spoke in the 1940s to fellow members in committee about training Africans for clerical posts in the municipal service a generation ahead of the time.
- At the same time, Rotarian Mr A Rancy reported to a committee on a proposal to staff Baragwanath Hospital almost completely with black people.
- In addition, Rotarian Mr Ray Philips criticised industry and commerce for not taking the unofficial trade unions more seriously, and appealed for help to gain official recognition. If this was not done, he said, the unions would be radicalised and be captured by the political left. Mr Philips believed employers should achieve official recognition for unions, for if they collapsed under pressure from the authorities and disappeared, it would be 25 years before they re-emerged with official blessing. In the event, it was 32 years before unions re-appeared.
- In 1948 the Non-European Affairs Committee of Rotary Johannesburg tried to win industry and commerce over to the United Nations Literacy Campaign, brought to South Africa by Dr F Laubach. Sponsors were not found and industry and commerce were largely indifferent. Now, 30 years later, many Rotary clubs and independent organisations are active in this field, using Dr Laubach's methods.

Directory of South African Rotary Clubs

There is a genetic basis to the care and concern we feel for our fellow men. We inherit a predisposition to help one another. This has arisen from the necessity for co-operative behaviour at the beginning of mankind's evolution. Competitive cultures tend to overlay and obscure the fact that there is a higher survival value in co-operation than in competition.

What occupies the foreground of our view of human nature today is derived mainly from ideas associated with the advent of the Industrial Revolution: highly individualistic, competing social actors carving a living or a profit while elbowing others out of the way. This perspective is not typical of the human condition. Almost 300 years have passed since the revolution in industry, which occupies a diminishing fraction of our history while the formative nature of our humanity was essentially forged millions of years ago.

The co-operative effort called forth to overcome large animals by a small, gracile proto-human was the moulding force in shaping our social nature. That and the long nurturing of the dependent infant, and the delay in maturing, is itself a design element in evolution for socialisation.

If co-operation and its companion, our feeling of compassion for the condition of others, is so deeply graven on the heart of mankind, then the work of service organizations is no more and no less than the natural expression of our human nature, albeit necessarily contained in some institutional guise. In a sense they have grown into service precisely to reaffirm our instinctive recognition that we are ordered by nature to care for one another.

How this manifests itself in particular instances among the 197 Rotary clubs in South Africa is a fascinating and rewarding study. The specific ways in which the Rotary sense of service is engaged, is amazingly varied, ranging from singular encounters with an individual need to broadly social engagements involving the environment and hundreds – even thousands – of people. This must be so. No matter how dense and diverse society is, it is composed of single, suffering fellow creatures calling on our fellowship.

No reflection is intended on other Rotary clubs when selecting one rather than another for particular mention. Each Rotary club and its committee members will vary in their evaluation of what constitutes the essence of the ideal of service in its particular community.

An interesting example is Louis Trichardt Rotary Club. The more familiar fund-raising projects are present, plus others with a tremendous social multiplier effect on environment, the quality of life and the cost to society at large.

In some rural areas a lack of water endangers the sight of infants. Fly and dust-borne infection of the eyes can often be reduced significantly by regular washing with clean water. Reduced water supplies make it difficult to apply this simple treatment. Unchecked infection causes tragic blindness among children. The introduction of an assured water supply to a settlement makes a dramatic difference in the lives of the people.

The Gazankulu black community is one such settlement in dire need of hygienic water. The Rotary Club of Louis Trichardt organized the surveying and planning of a pipeline with reservoirs from a fountain in nearby mountains. The planning done, the scheme was handed over to the community which, with the help of the local authority, undertook the project which was completed in 1984.

Throughout Africa the bulk of the rural population relies heavily on wood for fuel. Deforestation has become a major problem. The average African family consumes tons of firewood a year for domestic purposes. The women of each household walk further and further in search of fuel for daily meals. Often as much as five hours of each day can be spent in the search for timber – a serious drain on the economy of individual families.

Stripping of the woodlands degrades the grasslands, and therefore grazing leads to erosion and decreases soil fertility. The planting of suitable trees, fast-growing, easily coppiced and harvested, has multiplying beneficial effects on the community. The Louis Trichardt Rotary Club, with Dr P Jacques of Elim Hospital as project leader, co-ordinated planting trials of three varieties of a suitable species – Lucena or ipil-ipil. In several villages people were motivated to plant and care for the sapling trees. The experiment has been so successful that application has been made to the Rotary World Community Service Committee for registration of the project.

There are many comparable achievements in Rotary history in South Africa. A final example illustrates the scale of Rotary thinking. . . In 1928 Cape Town Rotary Club, using the model of the US, founded a Community Chest in Cape Town. In 1930, Durban Rotary Club formed the second Community Chest and since then Chests have been established in George, Uitenhage, Port Elizabeth, Pietermaritzburg, Empangeni and Springs. Pretoria and East London are in the process of setting up Chests.

In 1984 these Chests raised R4 500 000 for distribution to 320 welfare organisations: the blind and the deaf, the mentally retarded or handicapped, the aged, family and child welfare, youth services, epileptics, the jobless, TB patients, cripples, autistic children, rehabilitation of alcoholics, creches, etc.

The directory of Rotary clubs in South Africa which follows lists further projects and is a permanent and open window on conscience in the ideal of community service.

THE OBJECT OF ROTARY IS:

The development of acquaintance as an
opportunity for service.
High ethical standards in business
and professions;
the recognition of the worthiness
of all useful occupations;
each Rotarian using his occupation as an
opportunity to serve society.
The application of the ideal of service
by every Rotarian to his personal,
business and community life.
The advancement of international
understanding, goodwill and peace through
a world fellowship
of business and professional men united
in the ideal of service.

Rotary Clubs in South Africa

There are nearly 200 Rotary clubs in South Africa, functioning not only in the metropolitan areas, but also in the country districts. One common factor stands out – service based on care and concern for the well-being of others. Gauging the full extent and depth of this concern is hardly possible. Rather, it is that quality of Rotarians to recognise needs in their own communities, and act upon them, that inspires reverence.

The following is a list of clubs in South Africa (with the district number in parentheses). Where supplied by the clubs, condensed information on some of the projects is recorded. These are not necessarily the major or outstanding projects. The purpose is not to praise, but to convey that spirit so prevalent in the service of Rotarians.

ALBERTON (930)

Charter date: November 26, 1966
Charter president: Mr C Beyle-
veld
Projects:
- Establishment of a Golden Years Club for senior citizens.
- Donated a mini-bus for the Hamlet Organisation.

ALGOA BAY (932)

Charter date: April 16, 1958
Charter president: Dr P J Olivier
Projects:
- Heart of the Year Award (run in association with the South African Heart Foundation), given to the heart patient judged to have shown the greatest fortitude in overcoming a major cardiac arrest.
- A retirement village for black people at Zwide, Port Elizabeth. The project, undertaken together with the four other Rotary clubs in Port Elizabeth and the Ekuphumleni Association for the Care of the Black Aged, aims to provide shelter for the elderly who are being displaced by the breakdown of the traditional extended family units due to urbanization and modernization.
- Bursary schemes for needy students.
- Renovation of classrooms and a children's home in a black township.
- Renovation of offices of the Family and Marriage Society of South Africa.
- Renovation of Red Cross Clinic, South End.
- Sponsorship of Youth For Christ leadership course.

ALIWAL NORTH (932)

Charter date: April 10, 1978
Charter president: Mr C Mathews
Projects:
- Linking Rotary and World Vision to administer a feeding scheme for black and coloured school children in three towns in the area.
- Supplied a refrigerator for storing medicines to a mobile clinic in the area.

AMANZIMTOTI (927)

Charter date: June 19, 1965
Charter president: Dr L Roberts
Projects:
- Supports a school feeding scheme for local black children which involved the erection of school kitchens; and subsidises needy school children suffering from tuberculosis.
- Provision of equipment for the first African golf club at Umlazi, near Amanzimtoti.
- Funding of teacher training bursaries.
- Running of leadership courses for teenagers of all races.
- Erected classrooms at an overcrowded black school.
- In association with the SA National Tuberculosis Association involved in African School Garden Scheme.
- Provided a new ambulance for the SA Red Cross.

ARCADIA (932)

Charter date: August 15, 1961
Charter president: Mr H Whitfield
Projects:
- Initiated the first day-care centre in East London for coloured children, which today

accommodates 120 children. Also provided equipment.

- Started an educational fund for underprivileged and needy students which later became the Ted and Mabel Everitt Bursary Fund. To date financial assistance has been provided for 90 students.
- Started the Heart Foundation Rehabilitation Centre at East London's Frere Hospital.
- Refurbishing dormitories at children's home.
- Piloted the registration of hunger relief as a welfare organisation.
- Started Tape Aids for the Blind in the area.
- Provided Frere Hospital with a C.A.T. Scanner.

BARBERTON (925)
Charter date: November 8, 1945
Charter president: Mr C R Genis

BEACON BAY (932)
Charter date: October 11, 1973
Charter president: Mr J van Rooyen
Projects:
- Established Kennersley Park, an entertainment club for senior citizens.
- Erected bus shelters for local black commuters.
- Established a trust fund to sponsor attendance of students to the Veld & Vlei youth leadership camp.

BEAUFORT WEST (935)
Charter date: June 28, 1957
Charter president: Mr A Crawford
Projects:
- Provided additional class-rooms at local black school.
- Up-graded a local black community hall.
- Assistance to students of all races with books, uniforms, bursaries and loans, career guidance and sponsorships for Veld & Vlei and Youth Exchange programmes.
- Donated a billirubenometer for blood-testing of newborn babies to local hospital.

BEDFORDVIEW (930)
Charter date: June 1, 1971
Charter president: Mr N Payne
Projects:
- Distribution of Christmas hampers to the elderly and needy in the area.
- Involved in the development of a retirement village.
- Provided assistance in cash and manpower to organisation such as St John's Ambulance, the Johannesburg Children's Home, the Avril Elizabeth Home for the Handicapped.

BELLVILLE (935)
Charter date: April 30, 1954
Charter president: Mr G Consani

BENONI (930)
Charter date: April 23, 1928
Charter president: Mr A Moore
Projects:
- Erection of a black high school in nearby Daveyton.

- Raised funds for equipment for the Ryn Park Home for the Aged.
- Established a workshop for handicapped boys at the St Joseph's Mission in Manzini.

BENONI VAN RYN (930)
Charter date: June 9, 1972
Charter president: Mr F Lilford
Projects:
- Acquired and presented a suitable property to the Vita Nova Committee, part of the Cerebral Palsy Association, as a care centre for mentally handicapped children.
- Donated a computer to the School of Achievement, and a specially adapted one for use by children attending the Muriel Brand School for the Cerebral Palsied.
- Warmth for Winter – the distribution of blankets to the needy.
- Equipped a ward at Rynpark Senior Citizens Complex with special equipment and furniture.
- Quality of Life Project – assisting black businessmen in lectures and discussions with business management.

BETHAL (925)
Charter date: November 21, 1955
Charter president: Mr B J Havenga

BETHLEHEM (932)
Charter date: January 17, 1955
Charter president: Mr R van der Merwe
Projects:
- Established a youth hall at pleasure resort.
- Donated a mobile incubator for maternity unit (all races).
- Donated a TV and video to library for educational purposes.
- Distribute blankets to the needy.

BLOEMFONTEIN (past) (932)
Charter date: January 13, 1927
Charter president: Mr I Haarburger
Club terminated: March 17, 1931

BLOEMFONTEIN (932)
Charter date: April 14, 1950
Charter president: Mr J Reitz-Hofmeyer

BOKSBURG (930)
Charter date: August 1, 1938
Charter president: Mr J J Du Pre le Roux
Projects:
- Purchased, renovated and equipped a pair of semi-detached houses, and transferred them to the Good Companions Club for the Aged. This project received a Paul Harris Award.
- Established Bokkie Park, where city-born children can play among animals.
- Combined with other clubs to build a nursery at Modderbee Hospital for babies born of T.B. patients.
- Arrange annual holiday for senior citizens.

- Built Extension to ward at the Horizon Clinic, a hospital for alcoholics.

BOKSBURG LAKE (930)
Charter date: October 7, 1977
Charter president: Mr E Burgess
Projects:
- Donated agricultural implements to needy farmers for Operation Hunger.
- Arrange visits to Kruger National Park for under-privileged children.

BOTHAVILLE (932)
Charter date: October 9, 1973
Charter president: Mr W Travers
Projects:
- Building Rotaria, a village for senior citizens, which will ultimately comprise 24 living units and a dining hall.

BRAKPAN (930)
Charter date: June 24, 1940
Charter president: Mr V Ash

BRAMLEY (930)
Charter date: July 10, 1970
Charter president: Mr M Colman
Projects:
- Built two football fields in nearby black township of Alexandra.
- Built a primary school for black children at Alexandra.
- Built several schools in Lebowa.
- Involved in the establishment of a technical training institute in Alexandra at an estimated cost of R5 000 000.

BRITS (925)
Charter date: April 30, 1960
Charter president: Mr G Price

BUTTERWORTH (927)
Charter date: February 15, 1984
Charter president: Mr J Pedler

CALEDON (935)
Charter date: March 19, 1960
Charter president: Mr E Smit

CAPE OF GOOD HOPE (935)
Charter date: September 10, 1958
Charter president: Mr N Jeffes
Projects:
- Erected a toposcope at Cape Point.
- Established the Nerina Gardens Home for the Aged.
- Equipped a children's playground in the coloured township, Ocean View.
- Started and arranges annual Hospitality Holidays programme for senior citizens.
- Involved with school feeding programme.

CAPE TOWN (935)
Charter date: April 29, 1925
Charter president: Sir Carruthers Beattie
Projects:
- Founded the Community Chest of the Western Cape.
- Reconstructed premises at the former Rondebosch Cottage Hospital to house part of the Child Care Centre run by the Child Health Unit of the University of Cape Town.
- Established the Rotary Camp

Organisation at Glencairn, to enable under-privileged children to enjoy seaside holidays.
- Founded South Africa's first eye bank.
- Through the Birthday Scheme, provides about 600 gifts to children in various homes, institutions and orphanages on their birthdays.
- Initiated and participated in the founding of the Cape Flats Distress Association (CAFDA) to assist impoverished coloured communities on the Cape Flats.
- Established the Strandfontein Holiday Camp.

CARLETONVILLE (930)
Charter date: February 25, 1956
Charter president: Mr J Grolman
Projects:
- Established Rotara, a school for mentally handicapped children.
- Participated in the establishment of Senatus, a housing project for the aged comprising 73 units and a community centre.

CERES (935)
Charter date: June 6, 1985
Charter president: Mr K Pieters

CLAREMONT (935)
Charter date: October 10, 1974
Charter president: Mr S F Leng
Projects:
- Raised funds for the building of a creche in the coloured township of Hanover Park.

CLARENS (932)
Charter date: April 21, 1983
Charter president: Mr S Marriot

COLESBERG (932)
Charter date: September 3, 1966
Charter president: Mr A M van Niekerk
Projects:
- Donated medical equipment to Colesberg Hospital.
- Built a public swimming pool in Colesberg.
- Assisted the SA Red Cross with the furnishing of an old age home.

CONSTANTIA (935)
Charter date: October 21, 1978
Charter president: Mr B Hobbs
Projects:
- Designed and developed the Rokar, a hand-propelled car to provide mobility for children without the use of their legs.
- Assisted in establishing a nursery school in Guguletu, a black township in Cape Town.
- Provides wheelchairs and 'buggles' for the handicapped.
- Built a netball court at a school for children of farm labourers.
- Landscaped a playground and provided equipment to centre for the handicapped.

CRADOCK (932)
Charter date: October 2, 1959
Charter president: Mr H Becker
Projects:
- Erected a building in local black township for TB patients.
- Raising funds to build a senior citizens home in the area.
- Started school feeding scheme

and erected a building for this purpose.

DE AAR (932)
Charter date: May 14, 1958
Charter president: Mr M Liebenberg
Projects:
- Established the local branch of the Society for the Prevention of Cruelty to Animals (SPCA), and assisted with the erection of a building.
- Built additional classroom at local nursery school.
- Transporting of senior citizens from old age home to shops.

DRAKENSTEIN (935)
Charter date: August 25, 1983
Charter president: Mr P Muggeridge
Projects:
- Arrange Carols by Candlelight as an annual community service.
- Organise and host outings for children in children's home.

DURBAN (927)
Charter date: January 25, 1925
Charter president: Dr S G Campbell
Projects:
- Started the Community Chest of Durban.
- Launched the Aubrey Beiles Medical project, which provides short-wave radio communication between hospitals, clinics and ambulances throughout Natal/KwaZulu. This already elaborate project was accepted and expanded by the KwaZulu Government.

- Established the non-racial Lulama clinic for alcoholics.
- Manage a loan fund for students of all races.
- Established the Mnini holiday camp for black people.

DURBAN BAY (927)
Charter date: November 7, 1980
Charter president: Mr J Wood
Projects:
- Assisted with the establishment of a Citizen's Advice Bureau.
- Involved with the establishment of a clinic in KwaZulu.
- Raised funds for charity by organising and promoting an annual sports day between the Durban Chambers of Industry and Commerce.

DURBAN BEREA (927)
Charter date: March 20, 1971
Charter president: Mr M Hoyer
Projects:
- Administers international teacher exchange programme.
- Built a complex, the Zamazulu Nkosi Centre, comprising an old age home and day-care centre for the KwaMashu Christian Care Society.
- Donated mini-buses to Ematupeni Cripple Care Centre, to TAFTA (The Association for the Aged), and a mini-van to Meals-on-Wheels.
- Built the Inkonka Camp on the Umgeni Trust Game Farm, for the benefit of young people to learn to love and care for their natural heritage.
- Supported the establishment of the Warman House for young drug addicts.

DURBAN MUSGRAVE (927)

Charter date: March 24, 1978
Charter president: Mr J Fannin
Projects:

- Runs courses in basic business principles for black entrepreneurs; created local councils of Rotarians and black businessmen (Rotanda Councils) to promote the up-grading of business skills among black businessmen. Over the past 3-4 years more than 120 courses were held for over 2 000 businessmen.
- Built classrooms at the Mbibi School in KwaZulu.
- Embarked on a project to acquire land and raise funds for a home for black children in KwaMashu.
- Donated desks to Mcopheleli Higher Primary School.
- Built the Shelter Falls Camp at the Umgeni Valley Ranch where young people from the city are introduced to the joys of outdoor life and conservation.

DURBAN PORT NATAL (927)

Charter date: May 9, 1966
Charter president: Mr J Anderson
Projects:

- Built the Port Natal Community Centre in Durban, which provides full day care for 70 children of working mothers.
- Established and operates the Zululand Medical Scheme which flies medical specialists to mission hospitals in Zululand to advise hospital staff in rural areas. The scheme also provides transport for medical requirements such as crutches and bedding donated by the Club.
- Raising funds to build a pre-primary school for 160 black children.

DURBAN SOUTH (927)

Charter date: November 26, 1954
Charter president: Mr L Boyd
Projects:

- Built, equipped and stocked a library in the local black township of Umlazi.
- Runs a school-feeding scheme (Their Daily Bread Fund) at 63 local schools, feeding over 30 000 children every school day.
- At present building a home for senior citizens at Umlazi.
- Donated a 30-seater bus to TAFTA (The Association for the Aged).
- Together with Round Table No. 2, built Minitown on the Durban beachfront to raise funds for charity.

DURBAN UMGENI (927)

Charter date: August 8, 1977
Charter president: Mr Chips Jackson
Projects:

- Involved in a conservation project in the Durban Umgeni mangrove swamps, funding the erection of an information and research building, and supplying computer equipment.
- Actively involved with the Cheshire Home for Disabled Children in the local coloured community.
- Formed the first PROBUS Club in South Africa.

DURBAN UMHLATUZANA (927)
Charter date: September 8, 1979
Charter president: Mr N Dawber

DURBANVILLE (935)
Charter date: September 29,
1971
Charter president: Mr Bill Cherry
Projects:
- Supplied school desks as part
  of the Operation Up-grade programme.
- Arranged bi-annual careers information evenings at high
  schools in the area.
- Donated milking machine and
  work benches to Camphill Village.

EAST LONDON (932)
Charter date: April 2, 1926
Charter president: Mr B Myers
Projects:
- Supported the establishment
  of the Newhaven Home for the
  Chronically Sick.
- Providing housing and medical
  services to members of the local black, coloured and Asiatic
  communities.
- Established the D. J. Sobey
  Home for senior citizens, serving the local coloured community.
- Provides financial assistance
  to needy scholars and students
  of all races.
- Established a 'Solo Club' for di-
  vorced and lonely single per-
  sons.
- Established a holiday camp in
  the mountains near Hogsback
  enabling needy children to enjoy two weeks holiday.

EDENVALE (930)
Charter date: June 12, 1962
Charter president: Mr D Dickie
Projects:
- Started the Edenvale news-
  paper.
- Through Radio RSA started
  broadcasts to Rotarians in
  other countries.
- Piloted the establishment of
  the Edenvale Senior Citizens
  Centre.

ERMELO (925)
Charter date: May 17, 1950
Charter president: Mr J Stanton
Projects:
- Established the Swempec Hol-
  iday Home for Senior Citizens
  at Badplaas in the Eastern
  Transvaal in association with
  six other Rotary Clubs of Dis-
  trict 925.

ESHOWE (927)
Charter date: September 30,
1959
Charter president: Mr J R Ed-
wards
Projects:
- Actively involved with the establishment and work of the
  Eshowe Christian Action
  Group, a non-racial ecumenical
  body, which aims to supply ad-
  equate educational facilities in
  KwaZulu. More than 200 classrooms have been built since
  the establishment of the group
  in 1977.
- Produced a professional video
  on the work of the Eshowe
  Christian Action Group for local and overseas distribution.

ESTCOURT (927)
Charter date: March 16, 1966
Charter president: Mr G D B Forder

EVANDER (925)
Charter date: March 13, 1971
Charter president: Mr T Bosman

FICKSBURG (932)
Charter date: June 9, 1970
Charter president: Mr D Hyland
Projects:
- Presented courses on sales tax for local black businessmen.
- Sends matric scholars to Adventure into Citizenship, and underprivileged children on holiday to the sea.

GATELY (932)
Charter date: November 26, 1970
Charter president: Mr D Maclaren
Projects:
- Involved with the Malcomess Children's Home – and with the up-grading of the premises.
- Annual fundraising programme for the establishment of an old age home.

GEORGE (935)
Charter date: October 22, 1951
Charter president: Mr A Roberts
Projects:
- Raised funds for the rebuilding of the airport at Laingsburg which was extensively damaged by the floods in 1981.
- Established Rotary House for the local coloured community.
- Assisted in establishing the Red Cross air ambulance.

GERMISTON (930)
Charter date: October 2, 1929
Charter president: Mr W M Martin

GERMISTON NORTH (930)
Charter date: November 5, 1971
Charter president: Mr C Anderson
Projects:
- Established Rotary Village, a housing project for senior citizens.
- Donated desks and sports equipment to nearby black schools.
- Established an animal farm at the Avril Elizabeth Home for the mentally and physically handicapped.
- Donated a cardiac unit to the ambulance section of Germiston.
- Donated a bus to the Zimileni Home for mentally and physically handicapped children in Katlehong.

GOODWOOD (935)
Charter date: March 16, 1959
Charter president: Mr Sakkie van der Merwe
Projects:
- Established the Goodwood Handshake, a quarterly publication on South Africa, which ran from 1964 to 1970. Copies of the publication were distributed to Rotary clubs throughout the world.
- Supports the Peninsula School Feeding Association.
- Established clubs for senior citizens.
- Developed and maintains a handyman scheme which pro-

vides casual employment for pensioners in the area.
- Took over the Rokar Project from the Constantia Club and arranging their own manufacturing facilities.
- Organises fun holidays for senior citizens.

GRAAFF-REINET (932)
Charter date: March 27, 1957
Charter president: Mr A F Byrne
Projects:
- Launched a school feeding scheme during winter months for coloured and black children.
- Provided an intensive care unit at the local hospital.
- Started and manages a bursary fund for needy and deserving scholars of all races.

GRAHAMSTOWN (932)
Charter date: October 19, 1949
Charter president: Mr H Rushmere
Projects:
- Instrumental in establishing the local Brookshaw Home for the Aged.
- Provides transport for senior citizens to weekly meetings.
- Organises an annual Carols by Candlelight pageant to raise funds for charity.

GREENPARK (930)
Charter date: May 12, 1981
Charter president: Mr M Pike

GREYTOWN (927)
Charter date: May 4, 1974
Charter president: Mr Bill van Breda

Projects:
- Arranged a country fair to provide an opportunity for various charity, service, church and youth groups to raise funds.
- Built a shower block for general use at a local nature conservation ranch.

GROOTE SCHUUR (935)
Charter date: June 30, 1970
Charter president: Mr M M Sac

HARRISMITH (932)
Charter date: June 18, 1958
Charter president: Mr T Searle
Projects:
- Arranged and paid for the publication of a book The Story of Harrismith. Proceeds from sales of the book were used to establish a bursary fund for needy children.
- Supplied the local hospital with incubators for premature babies, an ECG unit and an iron lung.
- Revived local SPCA and built kennels and office accommodation.
- Established and equipped a playpark in the town.
- Supplied a coolroom, furniture, a piano and four tape recorders to the local old age home.

HEIDELBERG (930)
Charter date: June 14, 1961
Charter president: Mr O C Meek
Projects:
- Established a soup kitchen for local black pensioners.
- Provide Christmas hampers to needy people.
- Gives Christmas presents to

patients and staff of the hospital.
- Arrange accommodation and transport for the aged to the mineral spa at Badplaas.

HELDERBERG (935)
Charter date: May 17, 1983
Charter president: Mr J de Bruin
Projects:
- Supports Hottentots Holland Hospital on an on-going basis. Two resuscitation trollies have already been supplied.

HENNENMAN (932)
Charter date: November 3, 1960
Charter president: Mr Bill Grunow
Projects:
- Donated a bus to the local school, and an ambulance to the local town council.
- Contributes to a local fundraising project to establish a home for the town's senior citizens.
- Gives Christmas hampers to black pensioners every year.

HERMANUS (935)
Charter date: March 25, 1948
Charter president: Mr J de Villiers
Projects:
- Built a pre-primary school for local children.
- Donated life-saving equipment to the town council and established a local station of the National Sea Rescue Institute.
- Established the Camphill School for the mentally handicapped.
- Involved with a completed

housing project (18 double chalets and 8 single units) for the aged. Also involved with another project which will ultimately provide chalets, flats and rooms as well as a community centre and a geriatric unit for frail old people.
- Built a hall for Boy Scouts Troop.

HILLBROW (930)
Charter date: March 28, 1979
Charter president: Mr A Katz
Projects:
- Established The Forgotten Ones project, which provides emergency aid in the form of food, clothing and financial aid to people in the area.

HILLCREST (927)
Charter date: April 5, 1971
Charter president: Mr J Hopkins
Projects:
- Established an employment bureau for senior citizens.
- Built school desks for a local black school.
- Undertakes maintenance of building at local TB centre.
- Involved with upgrading of black teachers.
- Established Rotanda Council for the training of black businessmen.
- In conjunction with Wildlife Society, Lions and Round Table established Springside Nature Reserve.

HOWICK (927)
Charter date: January 19, 1970
Charter president: Mr T Catchpole

Projects:
- Donated a fully equipped ambulance to the local borough council.

ISIPINGO-PROSPECTON (927)
Charter date: November 20, 1980
Charter president: Mr Y Mohamed
Projects:
- Financially assists schools in Swaziland and KwaZulu.
- Built a kitchen for Enkesweni school.
- Provides clothing assistance to NICRO.
- Assists Durban Child Welfare Society.

JOHANNESBURG (930)
Charter date: July 1, 1921
Charter president: Mr H Hosken
Projects:
- Instrumental in establishing the Wilds Botanical Garden.
- Established a Citizen's Advice Bureau.
- Built Rotary Park, a senior citizens' housing project comprising 92 single units and eight double units.
- Supports adult education programmes in Soweto.
- Established a creche in the coloured township of Bosmont.
- Still runs a project started 63 years ago to entertain patients at the Johannesburg General Hospital with film shows. Two shows are presented every night by club members.
- Established and administers various educational trusts.

JOHANNESBURG EAST (930)
Charter date: March 18, 1968
Charter president: Mr H Wilkinson
Projects:
- Provided a language laboratory for Portuguese immigrants to learn English.
- Established the Soweto Child Minders, a scheme which provides care for children of working mothers.
- Provides financial support for the Avalon Home for Para- and Quadraplegics and donated a microcomputer to assist with administration and to provide electronic games for patients.
- Established Keurboom House, a home for cancer out-patients.
- Supplied borehole for mission hospital in KwaZulu.

JOHANNESBURG GOLDEN HIGHWAY (930)
Charter date: May 13, 1982
Charter president: Mr T Govindasami

JOHANNESBURG MAIN REEF (930)
Charter date: February 17, 1982
Charter president: Mr K Pretorius
Projects:
- Raised funds for beds in a new wing of the Ezibileni Home for crippled black children – a combined project with Edenvale Clinic.
- Provides financial support for the Avalon Home – a joint venture with two other clubs.

JOHANNESBURG NORTH CENTRAL (930)

Charter date: December 18, 1961
Charter president: Mr J Pitts
Projects:
- Established the Dorcas Day nursery for coloured children.
- Established the Holy Rosary School in the coloured township of Eldorado Park.
- Built two traffic training centres – one in Eldorado Park and the other at a Johannesburg school for the cerebral palsied.
- Raising funds for the development of a home for senior citizens in Soweto.

JOHANNESBURG SOUTH (930)

Charter date: November 22, 1968
Charter president: Mr R Attwell
Projects:
- Subsidises 16 scholars who attend Pace College in Soweto.
- Supports a self-help organisation for paraplegics and recently funded the visit of a member to the Bulova watch-making school in the USA.
- Instrumental in the re-housing of the Avalon Home in a new building complex.
- Donated 1 000 trees for a bird sanctuary in Soweto.
- Started five senior citizen clubs.

KEMPTON PARK (930)

Charter date: March 22, 1972
Charter president: Mr R D Wilson

KEMPTON PARK-JAN SMUTS (930)

Charter date: March 31, 1981
Charter president: Mr D Wilson
Projects:
- Established Operation Survival, a self-help scheme for unemployed people aimed at increasing their chances of employment by pooling resources and sharing skills and expertise.
- Launched Operation Wintercoat whereby overcoats are obtained from clubs in Europe and Canada for distribution to the needy such as newspaper vendors.

KILLARNEY (930)

Charter date: May 6, 1983
Charter president: Mr M Mealin
Projects:
- Established Operation Blindfold, a project for the importation of 3-dimensional copying machines enabling blind people to feel the outlines of photographs and drawings copied.

KIMBERLEY (932)

Charter date: August 20, 1951
Charter president: Mr E S Smith
Projects:
- Built a community centre and sports stadium in the black township of Galeshewe.
- Established Harmony Nursing Home for the chronically sick. It has 58 beds and 55 staff members.
- Established a youth hostel which provided more than 5 000 bed-nights in its first year.

KIMBERLEY SOUTH (932)
Charter date: December 3, 1970
Charter president: Mr N Dold
Projects:
- Presents courses for local black businessmen on administration, purchasing and marketing. Regular business seminars are also arranged in association with the National African Federated Chambers of Commerce (NAFCOC).
- Provides know-how in marketing, manufacturing, cash control and general business management to a local institution for the blind.
- Provided materials, guidance and assistance to the Taung community in Bophuthatswana to build a hospital complex on a self-help basis, complete with lecture hall, dining room, etc. Also provided equipment and furnishings.
- Initiated eye-testing scheme for under-privileged at Kimberley hospital.
- Donates tinned milk powder on a monthly basis to the Galeshewe Day Clinic and the Child Welfare Organisation for the benefit of malnourished children.
- Donated TV sets to children's hospital.
- Established a complete playground at Yonder, a home for mentally retarded people.

KING WILLIAM'S TOWN (932)
Charter date: January 24, 1950
Charter president: Mr E A Thompson
Projects:
- Purchased a bus for transporting children from King Wil- liams' Town to attend McLennand School for Retarded Children in East London.
- Active in a programme to support and entertain senior citizens.

KIRSTENBOSCH (935)
Charter date: June 10, 1985
Charter president: Mr P Evans-Watt

KLERKSDORP (932)
Charter date: 23 November 1953
Charter president: Mr H Wood
Projects:
- Started Rota Park, a housing complex for local senior citizens. To date 63 homes, a block of four flats and a community hall have been completed.
- Established an interest-free loan scheme for local students of all races.

KLOOF (927)
Charter date: June 26, 1980
Charter president: Mr O Kealton
Projects:
- Funded the visit to the USA of a teacher for the deaf. Plans an exchange scheme between deaf students from South Africa and the USA.
- Started a project to establish a retirement village.

KNYSNA AND PLETTENBERG BAY (935)
Charter date: May 4, 1962
Charter president: Mr R Gordon
Projects:

- Donated a light truck to Knysna Child Welfare.
- Offers swimming lessons to children from coloured communities.
- Raises funds to supply additional accommodation at Veld & Vlei camp at Sedgefield.
- Presented a resuscitation unit for cardiac patients to local hospital.

KOKSTAD (927)
Charter date: June 20, 1972
Charter president: Rev W E Burgess

KROONSTAD (932)
Charter date: May 19, 1959
Charter president: Mr G Holmes
Projects:
- Established a scheme to distribute meat and other necessities to old and indigent black people.
- Donated funds to extend a local creche for coloured children.
- Toys for Joy – collects toys through white schools for distribution to children in black and coloured communities at Christmas.

KRUGERSDORP (930)
Charter date: September 9, 1940
Charter president: Mr G Breytenbach

KRUGERSDORP MONUMENT (930)
Charter date: September 16, 1982
Charter president: Mr G Engelbrecht
Projects:
- Supplied food, toys and books to a mission clinic in Lebowa.
- Provided plans for the local Cripple Care Organisation's new centre.
- Bought two houses to house out-patients of local mental hospital.

KURUMAN (932)
Charter date: September 9, 1965
Charter president: Mr A Faur
Projects:
- Built a pavilion, and donated a piano and film projectors to the local high school.
- Provided and fitted panel heaters at hospital.

KYALAMI (930)
Charter date: March 9, 1981
Charter president: Mr S Lipschitz
Projects:
- Financed the supply and installation of an engine driven pump and borehole equipment at a remote village in Botswana.
- Sponsored a South African lecture tour by a UK specialist on Downe's Syndrome.
- Funded the visit to South Africa and the hospitalisation and rehabilitation of a patient from Malawi who was fitted with two artificial arms.
- Built a swimming pool at Cluny Farm, a residence and place of work for mentally handicapped youths.

LADYSMITH (927)
Charter date: August 29, 1949
Charter president: Mr H L Kidman
Projects:
- Provided boreholes in drought-stricken areas.
- Donates equipment to local black schools, and to Cripple Care Association.

LION'S HEAD (935)
Charter date: February 9, 1980
Charter president: Mr J Powell
Projects:
- Ran Road Courtesy Campaign.

LOMBARDY (930)
Charter date: June 1, 1984
Charter president: Mr G Bray

LOUIS TRICHARDT (925)
Charter date: February 19, 1959
Charter president: Mr I Torrance
Projects:
- Established a bursary fund for needy scholars of all races.
- Surveyed and planned a water scheme to serve a black community in Gazankulu.
- Initiated and organised trial plantings of suitable trees for woodlots in Ganzankulu. (The success of this project has led its initiator to apply for it to be registered as a World Community Service project.)

MAFIKENG (930)
Charter date: June 18, 1958
Charter president: Mr W Steyn
Projects:
- Erected and established the Rotarus Home for senior citizens.

- Established the Mafikeng Museum.
- Built a playground for local coloured children.
- Organises careers information exhibitions for Bophuthatswana scholars.

MALMESBURY (935)
Charter date: April 22, 1954
Charter president: Mr P C van der Merwe

MARGATE (927)
Charter date: August 5, 1950
Charter president: Mr A W O'Connor

MEYERTON/HENLY ON KLIP (930)
Charter date: June 16, 1975
Charter president: Mr J G Dickinson

MIDDELBURG (925)
Charter date: November 19, 1956
Charter president: Mr I J Rosser
Projects:
- Provided an ambulance for use in the local black township.
- Introduced a milk-feeding scheme for local children.
- Provided playground equipment to local coloured township.
- Provided fire-fighting equipment for Kruger National Park.
- Runs annual art competition at local high schools.
- Presented 'Jaws-of-Life' to local municipality.

MILNERTON (935)
Charter date: June 6, 1977
Charter president: Mr J de Villiers

MOOI RIVER (927)
Charter date: September 11, 1970
Charter president: Mr V Kinsman
Projects:
- Erected a farm school for black children in the nearby Drakensberg mountains.

MOSSEL BAY (935)
Charter date: October 30, 1952
Charter president: Mr M Elion
Projects:
- Initiated the establishment of Ons Tuis, a home for senior citizens.
- Contributed funds for an air ambulance and for a vessel for the National Sea Rescue Institute.
- Started preparations to establish and build a second old age home.

NELSPRUIT (925)
Charter date: March 24, 1952
Charter president: Mr Bob Aling
Projects:
- Runs an inter-schools quiz competition.
- Takes senior citizens on holidays to Kruger National Park.

NELSPRUIT JOCK (925)
Charter date: October 18, 1982
Charter president: Mr D Pretorius
Projects:
- Financial aid to a local home for mentally handicapped children, as well as to Child Welfare.

NEWCASTLE (927)
Charter date: December 2, 1966
Charter president: Mr F Hemingway
Projects:
- Arranged a multi-racial symposium on the future of Greater Newcastle and sold all 600 seats at R10 per head.
- Erected a creche in the nearby black township of Madadeni.
- Established an interest-free loan for black students.

NEWCASTLE-MAJUBA (927)
Charter date: May 14, 1976
Charter president: Mr W Klingenberg
Projects:
- Established an annual careers advisory service for black and Indian students and provides financial assistance for university students.
- Initiated and co-ordinated a fund-raising campaign to buy an ambulance for the local branch of the S.A. Red Cross.

NEW GERMANY-WESTVILLE (927)
Charter date: August 23, 1969
Charter president: Mr C J van Hoften
Projects:
- Built the KwaDabeka Home for 150 black senior citizens.
- Built two science classrooms for a local black high school and a classroom at a black farm school.

- Established a feeding scheme for unemployed black people.
- Started a bursary scheme for top science and mathematics students at a local black high school.
- Training middle management of all races in aptitude testing for the placement of workers with minimum skills.

NIGEL (930)

Charter date: April 3, 1939
Charter president: Mr A V Sheldon
Projects:

- Established a scholar care centre.
- Provide blankets to the poor.

NORTHCLIFF (930)

Charter date: May 16, 1973
Charter president: Mr W Klemptner
Projects:

- Established and supervises a self-help development programme in the black village of Maserula in the North Western Transvaal. This includes, amongst others, the building of classrooms, the installation of a borehole and the running of an agricultural project.
- Established a creche for 60 children in a nearby coloured township.
- Donated laboratory and library equipment to several local black schools.

NORTH DURBAN (927)

Charter date: February 10, 1960
Charter president: Mr W Meyers
Projects:

- Initiated and co-ordinated the establishment of the Mental Health Industrial Training Centre.
- Established the Old Friends' Club.
- Established an art centre in KwaMashu.

- Provided a swimming pool and playground for the William Clark Gardens Project for Spastics.
- Initiated and co-ordinates a self-help water provision scheme in the informal settlements outside Durban involving the community concerned and the Sugar Association. Financial support is received from District 971 in Australia.

ODENDAALRUS (932)

Charter date: August 1, 1960
Charter president: Mr B Regal
Projects:

- Established a milk-feeding scheme for blacks in outlying rural areas.
- Provides financial assistance to the dependants of TB patients.
- Established a nursery school for black children, and assisted four black mothers to establish creches.
- Donated books and sports equipment to local black high schools.
- Built a road-safety training ground for children.

ORANGE GROVE (930)
Charter date: July 28, 1955
Charter president: Mr W Frankish
Projects:
- Laid foundation for the establishment of the South African Paraplegic Games Association.
- Built and runs a tea kiosk at The Wilds to raise funds for charity.

ORKNEY (932)
Charter date: January 7, 1959
Charter president: Mr A Kruger

OUDTSHOORN (935)
Charter date: November 12, 1955
Charter president: Mr I Kahn
Projects:
- Established a loan scheme for local students.
- Donated medical equipment to the local hospital.
- Built a bungalow at Mossel Bay and arranged holidays for groups of under-privileged children.

PAARL (935)
Charter date: June 27, 1940
Charter president: Mr J F Knott-Craig

PAROW (935)
Charter date: September 6, 1966
Charter president: Mr E Sacks
Projects:
- Established a creche for local children.
- Established a senior citizen employment service.
- Donated a motor vehicle to the community workers in a local coloured township.

- Provided furniture and fittings for Nxolo school at Cross-roads.

PARYS (932)
Charter date: June 23, 1955
Charter president: Mr T Gradwell
Projects:
- Established a bursary fund for deserving local students.
- Provides financial assistance for the building of an old age home.
- Sends children on holiday to the coast.
- Built a holiday camp near the Vaal River.

PIET RETIEF (927)
Charter date: May 12, 1960
Charter president: Mr D E Cutter
Projects:
- Assisted in a combined Rotary project to build a holiday resort for senior citizens.
- Built a roller-skating rink for the youth of the town.

PIETERMARITZBURG (927)
Charter date: March 12, 1925
Charter president: Mr H Brian
Projects:
- Establishing a bursary fund for needy students.
- Provided materials to erect water reservoirs in KwaZulu.
- Distributes Christmas hampers to needy black people (ongoing for 40 years.)

PIETERMARITZBURG AZALEA (927)
Charter date: February 19, 1982
Charter president: Mr F Maytham

PIETERMARITZBURG EAST (927)
Charter date: November 1, 1969
Charter president: Mr A Tarr
Projects:
- Actively involved in the local hospital's craniofacial unit, funding treatment for needy patients, and providing equipment.
- Established a scheme which will provide teachers to train black youths in the practical work of a variety of trades, businesses and professions.
- Erected a science laboratory at a nearby black school, and raised funds to build classrooms at several black schools.

PIETERSBURG (925)
Charter date: May 15, 1951
Charter president: Mr W C Marsh
Projects:
- Raising funds and overseeing the upgrading and extension of St Brendan's Clinic, which provides a 24-hour medical service, 7 days a week to the impoverished agrarian Batlokwa people.

PIETERSBURG CAPRICORN (925)
Charter date: September 11, 1977
Charter president: Mr B Lavers
Projects:
- Annual excursions for needy pensioners to holiday resort.

PINETOWN (927)
Charter date: October 12, 1953
Charter president: Mr D Timm
Projects:
- Assisted with the establishment of three housing projects for senior citizens.
- Established the Old Mill Sports and Social Club at Marianhill. This multi-racial centre, which is used by over 10 000 people a month, provides sporting and recreational facilities, as well as a creche and self-help industries.
- Built 11 classrooms in the black township of Clermont.

PINETOWN CENTRAL
Charter date: March 3, 1975
Charter president: Mr D Shave

PORT ALFRED (927)
Charter date: March 22, 1985
Charter president: Mr P Leach
Projects:
- Cleaning up Kowie River and environment.

PORT ELIZABETH (932)
Charter date: April 26, 1925
Charter president: Mr T C White
Projects:
- Erected a creche at the nearby Windvogel coloured township.
- Distributed dictionaries to 12 local black high schools in conjunction with the Butte Rotary Club, Montana, USA.
- Toys for Joy: manufactures toys for distribution to underprivileged children.

PORT ELIZABETH EAST (932)
Charter date: November 25, 1977
Charter president: Mr D Cleary
Projects:
- Organised games for disabled athletes.
- Constructed kitchen cupboards at children's home.

PORT ELIZABETH SOUTH (932)
Charter date: December 24, 1972
Charter president: Mr T P Grylls

PORT ELIZABETH WEST (932)
Charter date: April 19, 1969
Charter president: Mr A F Moss
Projects:
- Produced exercise books for black school children from donated paper.
- With the other Port Elizabeth Rotary clubs, assists in the building of a senior citizens' village for black people.
- Provided cane bending equipment for blind workers.
- Converted double-decker bus into playrooms for creche.
- Provided vehicles for Meals-on-Wheels project.

PORT SHEPSTONE (927)
Charter date: December 16, 1950
Charter president: Mr N I Bamber
Projects:
- Motivated the local authorities to establish a technical school in southern Natal.
- Assisted in building a sanatorium for tuberculosis patients.

POTCHEFSTROOM (932)
Charter date: June 9, 1948
Charter president: Mr C C McInnes

POTGIETERSRUS (925)
Charter date: July 11, 1961
Charter president: Mr C J Scheepers
Projects:
- Established a bursary fund for students of all races.
- Assisted with the building of accommodation for pupils of the Trans Oranje School for the Deaf at a holiday resort.

PRETORIA (925)
Charter date: August 6, 1925
Charter president: Mr H W Adams
Projects:
- Established the Castle Carey Home for the rehabilitation of alcoholics and drug dependants.
- Established a senior citizens home in the local coloured community.
- Established an autistic unit at a local school for the cerebral palsied.
- Established a dental clinic for the indigent.
- Established the Advice to Black Entrepeneurs Forum.

PRETORIA EAST (925)
Charter date: March 28, 1961
Charter president: Mr J Vorster
Projects:
- Piloted and co-ordinated extensive renovations and extentions to a senior citizens home for coloured people. (This is a joint venture with other Rotary clubs.)
- Built a swimming pool, bowling greens and clubhouse for blind bowlers.
- Built a Scout hall.

■ Donated new beds to an orphanage.

PRETORIA MAGALIESBERG (925)
Charter date: May 20, 1970
Charter president: Mr M D Click

PRETORIA SILVERTON (925)
Charter date: May 3, 1971
Charter president: Mr W E Fendick

PRETORIA 6 (925)
Charter date: October 7, 1981
Charter president: Mr E Murdock
Projects:
■ Establishing a community centre for local senior citizens.
■ Donated a vehicle to the Zodwa Training Centre for black people.
■ Provides funds to a training centre for the blind.
■ Holds annual career seminars for local black, coloured and Indian school communities.
■ Established Halfway House – a facility for patients of Weskoppies (a hospital for the mentally ill) to undergo an adaptation process before reintroduction as full members of society.

PRETORIA WEST (925)
Charter date: July 7, 1959
Charter president: Mr H Besaans

QUEENSTOWN (932)
Charter date: October 12, 1953
Charter president: Mr R Martin

RAADZAAL (932)
Charter date: May 20, 1970
Charter president: Mr Sam Saunders
Projects:
■ Piloted and co-ordinated the building of an interim home for patients receiving treatment for cancer.
■ Bought and equipped a mobile resuscitation unit for the local hospital.
■ Raised funds for the establishment of a cardiac rehabilitation centre at the local hospital.

RANDBURG (930)
Charter date: April 2, 1972
Charter president: Mr J Breytenbach
Projects:
■ Etablished the Water for Life project in a village in Lebowa. This entailed providing wells, pumps, storage tanks and reticulation in the village.
■ Assisted with renovations of the old premises of the Sunshine Centre for Retarded Children. Donated equipment and toys after the Centre moved to new premises.

RANDFONTEIN (930)
Charter date: August 16, 1943
Charter president: Mr S A Hendrikz

RICHARDS BAY (927)
Charter date: November 26, 1983
Charter president: Mr J Batho
Projects:
■ Planning the establishment of a home for young people and, under YMCA guidance, a holi-

day refuge for under-privileged children.

ROGGEBAAI (935)
Charter date: January 8, 1968
Charter president: Mr T Unite
Projects:
- Established a local seniors club.
- Donated a van to Meals-on-Wheels project.
- Runs an annual garden competition in Manenberg, a coloured township on the Cape Flats.

RONDEBOSCH (935)
Charter date: December 8, 1958
Charter president: Dr B Bromilow-Downing
Projects:
- Donating sports equipment to coloured youth clubs.
- Erected a community hall for use by local organisations.
- Providing a roof for a self-help centre at a home for the mentally handicapped.
- Built an all-weather playground at orphanage in coloured community.
- Arranges seaside trips for cripples at Maitland Cottage Hospital over Christmas period.
- Donated an ambulance to the St John's Organisation.
- Assists Operation Up-grade which teaches illiterate people to read and write.

ROODEPOORT (930)
Charter date: October 5, 1944
Charter president: Mr R van Niekerk
Projects:
- Established Florama, a home for senior citizens.
- Provided tape recorders to eight blind members of the community and subscribed on their behalf to Tape Aids for the Blind.
- Provided furniture and books for library in coloured community.
- Donated two kidney machines to Discoverer's Hospital.

ROODEPOORT CENTRAL (930)
Charter date: November 11, 1974
Charter president: Mr R Sack

ROSEBANK (930)
Charter date: June 16, 1954
Charter president: Dr J Boswell
Projects:
- Built a nursery school, and equipped the library of a primary school in the black township of Alexandra. Thousands of books were donated by clubs from all over the world.
- Donating funds to a college in Lebowa.
- Built Montgomery Haven, a home for 62 senior citizens.

RUSTENBURG (925)
Charter date: December 16, 1950
Charter president: Mr F W Offermeier

SABIE (925)
Charter date: July 23, 1982
Charter president: Mr B Pappin

SALDANHA (935)
Charter date: March 25, 1965
Charter president: Mr S Levin
Projects:

- Built the Diasville Clinic in a nearby coloured township.
- Established a Spanish library for the Spanish-speaking residents of the town.
- Runs an annual toy-making project for under-privileged children.
- Donated money to Huis Wittekruin (an old age home) and landscaped its gardens.

SANDTON (930)
Charter date: June 8, 1970
Charter president: Mr J Ferguson
Projects:

- Built classrooms, donated desks and supplied a borehole and piping for a black farm school.
- Established temporary accommodation and a recreation centre for senior citizens in the black township of Alexandra. Completed the first phase of a permanent old age home to accommodate 2 300 people.

SANDOWN (930)
Charter date: August 14, 1984
Charter president: Mr M Daffy

SASOLBURG (930)
Charter date: August 9, 1963
Charter president: Mr E Doubell
Projects:

- Supports various local charity organisations.

SCOTTBURGH (927)
Charter date: June 5, 1957
Charter president: Mr S Jackson
Projects:

- Established a district clinic for black patients in the area. Also supplied equipment and medicine.
- Provided playing fields for local coloured school.
- Undertakes the selling of baskets on behalf of the Natal Society for the Blind during holiday periods.
- Provided piped music at hospital, and radios for use by patients.

SEA POINT (935)
Charter date: January 19, 1961
Charter president: Mr H Getz
Projects:

- Established a local office of Suicides Anonymous, now Life Line.
- Initiated and spearheaded a fund-raising drive among Rotary clubs to buy an air ambulance for use in the Western Cape. This became a Rotary District project.
- Equipped the library of a black school in Cape Town.
- Donated equipment to the haemotology department of Cape Town's Groote Schuur Hospital.
- Started 'Operation Allergy Disks', motivating members of the public allergic to certain medicines to wear wrist disks identifying their allergies.

SIGNAL HILL (935)
Charter date: May 7, 1971
Charter president: Mr S Paddock
Projects:
- Started the Rotary International Community Service Project for the supply of drugs and other medical requirements to a Salvation Army hospital in Zambia.
- Provides financial aid, medical and agricultural equipment to neighbouring black countries.
- Built a pre-primary classroom for a black school near Cape Town.
- Built a swimming pool for the blind and partially sighted in a coloured residential area near Cape Town.

SOMERSET WEST (935)
Charter date: August 15, 1955
Charter president: Mr J Strassheim
Projects:
- Established two homes for local senior citizens, Robari Home and Vonke Huis.
- Initiated a drive to establish a local nature reserve and donated the entrance gates.
- Established Operation Medical Exchange, bringing doctors from neighbouring black countries to study at the cardiac unit of Cape Town's Groote Schuur Hospital.

SPRINGS (930)
Charter date: July 17, 1935
Charter president: Mr J C Laight
Projects:
- Spearheaded the establishment of South Africa's largest settlement for tuberculosis patients.

- Planning a Rotary Village in the town for local senior citizens.
- Since 1943 have arranged annual multi-racial dinners for matriculants.

SPRINGS PARK (930)
Charter date: June 20, 1978
Charter president: Mr T Horwood
Projects:
- Established a playground for black children at the Far East Rand hospital.

STANDERTON (930)
Charter date: January 31, 1952
Charter president: Mr A W T Adams

STANGER (927)
Charter date: September 5, 1978
Charter president: Mr J E Heritage

STELLENBOSCH (935)
Charter date: April 14, 1937
Charter president: Mr T Louw
Projects:
- Started a utility company to erect 36 houses for senior citizens.

STRAND (935)
Charter date: June 22, 1953
Charter president: Mr A Friedman
Projects:
- Established a centre for the handicapped.
- Established a local technical college.
- Supports a school feeding scheme.
- Built tidal pool for children.

STUTTERHEIM (932)
Charter date: March 19, 1979
Charter president: Rev Bill Campbell
Projects:
- Established a social activities centre for local senior citizens.
- Established a pensioners' discount scheme among local businesses.

SWELLENDAM (935)
Charter date: November 6, 1965
Charter president: Mr E Morkel
Projects:
- Among others, actively involved in caring for the aged.

TABLE BAY (935)
Charter date: July 20, 1955
Charter president: Mr J Vivian
Projects:
- Provided an all-weather playground, sports ground, a nursery school and a children's centre for nearby coloured communities.
- Runs a school feeding programme, the Peninsula School Feeding Association, in Cape Town which provides a main meal for about 160 000 children every school day.
- Donated playground equipment to the Eros Cerebral Palsy school.
- Influenced local authority to undertake the necessary renovations of most of the houses in Maitland Garden Village. The club then improved the recreation areas, planted trees and constructed a creche. Also organised the formation of a Village Residents' Association.

- Initiated and co-ordinated the conversion of an industrial dump into a recreational area with lawns and trees for factory workers.

TAFELBERG (935)
Charter date: April 13, 1982
Charter president: Mr J Winchester
Projects:
- Undertook the trail-marking of the numerous walks and hikes on Table Mountain and in the Kirstenbosch Botanical Gardens.

THREE RIVERS (930)
Charter date: September 28, 1984
Charter president: Mr R Maguire

TZANEEN (925)
Charter date: June 27, 1961
Charter president: Mr A J E Funke

UITENHAGE (932)
Charter date: October 8, 1947
Charter president: Mr J L Nicholson
Projects:
- Established a school feeding scheme for local children.
- Established a blood transfusion centre.
- Establishing an intensive care unit at the local hospital.

UITENHAGE SOUTH (932)
Charter date: October 7, 1974
Charter president: Mr L Swift
Projects:
- Cash donations to various charity organisations.

UMHLANGA (927)
Charter date: April 9, 1973
Charter president: Mr J Rowe

UMTATA (927)
Charter date: January 17, 1949
Charter president: Mr H T Cocks
Projects:
- Renovated a local TB clinic.
- Established an educational fund.

UPINGTON (935)
Charter date: May 15, 1956
Charter president: Mr C Grobler
Projects:
- Established an old age home, and recently provided a mini-bus.

UVONGO (927)
Charter date: October 13, 1980
Charter president: Mr H Baekee
Projects:
- Established the Sibambisene Rotanda Council, comprising three Rotary clubs and the African Chamber of Commerce. The council holds regular seminars for black businessmen on book-keeping, banking, taxation and allied subjects.

VANDERBIJLPARK (930)
Charter date: March 26, 1956
Charter president: Mr P R Nell
Projects:
- Provided accommodation, clothing, work and language classes for Hungarian refugees.
- Erected and supplying the Manna clinic for the local black community.
- Established a home for local senior citizens.
- Provided a playground and swimming pool for local black children.
- Financed and assisted in building a hospital for the local SPCA.

VEREENIGING (930)
Charter date: September 25, 1944
Charter president: Mr A Snijman
Projects:
- Established a home for local senior citizens.
- Involved in the launching of the Vaal Show, an annual trade and agricultural show.
- Provides blankets for the needy in Sharpeville.

VILJOENSKROON (932)
Charter date: April 20, 1959
Charter president: Mr M Reid
Projects:
- Built a mortuary for local black people.
- Built four homes for senior citizens with plans for a further two.

VIRGINIA (932)
Charter date: August 19, 1959
Charter president: Mr J A Taljaard

VRYBURG (932)
Charter date: January 3, 1955
Charter president: Mr G J J Vlok

VRYHEID (927)
Charter date: May 3, 1961
Charter president: Mr W Wessels

WALVIS BAY (935)
Charter date: November 26, 1958
Charter president: Mr J H Newman
Projects:
- Provided X-Ray unit for the Cottage Hospital.
- Established a study loan scheme.

WARMBATHS (925)
Charter date: May 10, 1962
Charter president: Mr P Clarke
Projects:
- Equipped a creche for local black children and helped with a feeding scheme.
- Donated a heart monitoring machine and an incubator to a local missionary hospital.
- Established a university bursary fund for black students.
- Founded and sponsors senior citizens club.

WELKOM (932)
Charter date: April 1, 1955
Charter president: Mr A C Burge

WELKOM FLAMINGO (932)
Charter date: October 22, 1975
Charter president: Mr A Williams
Projects:
- Collects and distributes Christmas food parcels.

WELLINGTON (935)
Charter date: April 7, 1960
Charter president: Mr F C Brand
Projects:
- Makes a bequeathed house available for under-privileged children.

WESTONARIA (930)
Charter date: November 17, 1965
Charter president: Mr Bob McKenzie
Projects:
- Offers English classes for immigrants.

WESTVILLE (927)
Charter date: March 27, 1982
Charter president: Mr S Bloch
Projects:
- Joined with other local service organisations to provide a fully equipped hall for the Dawncliffe Home for retired people.

WHITE RIVER (925)
Charter date: May 9, 1956
Charter president: Mr J Barker
Projects:
- Established a bursary loan fund for local students.
- Built a sports pavilion for the local primary school.
- Established the local library.
- Established a bird sanctuary.
- Donated technical and sports equipment to old age home and numerous schools.

WINCHESTER HILLS (930)
Charter date: October 31, 1978
Charter president: Mr L Knight
Projects:
- Established a traffic unit at a cerebral palsy school.
- Sponsored the participation of paraplegics from a local black school to the South African Paraplegic games. Also built a playground unit.
- Administers a medical assistance scheme for foreign black workers in South Africa.
- Provided a borehole for a village in Transkei.
- Arranges Easter parties, picnics and food parcels for the aged.

WITBANK (925)
Charter date: March 1, 1954
Charter president: Mr T L Robb

WITBANK COALFIELDS (925)
Charter date: November 24, 1982
Charter president: Mr P Rademan

WORCESTER (935)
Charter date: November 2, 1946
Charter president: Mr H G Walters
Projects:
- Established the Worcester Cripple Care Association, and an orthopaedic clinic in the town.
- Established the Van Riebeeck Homes for the Aged.
- Established a local branch of Alcoholics Anonymous.
- Built the Rotary Service Centre.
- Established a complete Trim Park.

WYNBERG (935)
Charter date: December 12, 1949
Charter president: Mr N Jeffes
Projects:
- Founded the first club for senior citizens in Cape Town.
- Arranges career guidance evenings at local high schools.
- Involved in the development of the Nyanga Art Centre which provides facilities for activities such as pottery, woodwork and needlework classes, and dancing. It also incorporates a creche.
- Instrumental in establishing a training centre for epileptics which provides for about 4 000 epileptics in the Cape Peninsula.